SHORTS

FACT & FICTION

a collection of short stories

by

Doug Wicken

ISBN
Paperback: 978-0-9691228-6-9
eBook:: 978-0-9691228-7-6

Published by Doug Wicken, 2024

SHORTS (Fact & Fiction) includes works of both fiction and factual accounts based upon the author's personal memories, observations, and imagination. Names, characters, places, and incidents are the product of the author's imagination and are used fictitiously. Any resemblance to actual events, locales, or persons, living or dead, is entirely coincidental. In factual stories some names of real persons and places are used for the sole purpose of historical accuracy. No judgemental attempt is intended.

Warning
This work contains mention of the subjects of sexual assault and suicide. The incidents are intended only as references and do not contain graphic description. Misogynist words and phrases appear in some dialogue. They appear only to reflect the speaker's attitudes and a specific time and place.

Cover image by Tsokur, iStock.com
Interior photos © Doug Wicken
Photograph of the author by Scott Wicken at Café O.
Formatting by Chrissy Hobbs at Indie Publishing Group Inc

DEDICATION

I dedicate this collection to Gudrun Hedwig Heiss. She has always referred to me as a teller of tales and has a special fondness for my short stories.

It is also dedicated to the memory of Joy Middleton (1963 – 2022). She lived in a small world, but her smiles and unselfish joy were contagious to us all.

(see An Ode to Joy)

ACKNOWLEDGEMENTS

Many thanks to freelance editor, Catherine Muss, who has guided me through the editing process. Her sharp eyes and encouragements have made this collection much better than originally imagined. Most, but not all, of her valuable suggestions have been followed.

A very special thanks to fellow author, Lindsey-Anne Pontes (DeSousa), a trusted and helpful reader, friend, and source of publishing information. She has unselfishly volunteered her time and knowledge to my writing projects.

Thanks to Chrissy Hobbs of Indie Publishing Group for her valued assistance with the formatting and design.

To Irina and the wonderful staff (Abigail, Brooke, Hope, Kadence, Kendra, Mark, Miranda, Stacie, Zahra, and others) at Café O in Kitchener, Ontario, my all-time favourite café and writing space.

To the regulars at Café O, particularly those who have shared their wisdom and conversation with me and who have accommodated my endless rants and relentless philosophical meanderings: Mamoon Chakhansuri, Deborah Polzin, Lindsey-Anne Pontes (DeSousa).

To all of my fellow writers of Kitchener-Waterloo Writers Alliance for their camaraderie, advice, and encouragement to experienced and novice writers alike. Thanks especially to those who have volunteered to read my work in progress and have offered valuable advice: Maureen Duffy, Amy Prendergast, Jody Swannell, Bill Van Dyk, and Drea Cohane.

A very special thanks to my loving family:
Scott Wicken, Shelley Young, and Rowan;
Craig and Nena Wicken, Luka and Gabrijela (Brie);
Gudrun Heiss

And to my dear special friend, Sher Kariz.

CONTENTS

WELCOME

Welcome to ***SHORTS (Fact & Fiction)***, my collection of short stories that has been 80-plus years in the making. This is not, of course, to suggest that I've been writing them for 80-plus years, but that they represent inspirations that have been accumulating for that long.

The collection is a blend of both fictional and non-fictional accounts of events and imaginations that have travelled through my mental hard drive, a collaboration between the left and right channels of my cerebral cortex.

The fine line separating the factual from the fictional, however, is more akin to scanning the landscape from the tip of my nose to infinity through a pair of progressive eyeglass lenses; a line too fine, in some cases, for even my own memory to discern.

Although I have engaged in some fascinating occupations, my life overall has been neither exceptional nor adventurous; quite the opposite in fact. Even an agoraphobic who dwells within the confines of a small, darkened apartment is capable of creating the most exciting prose, whether as fact or fiction, based solely upon their own experiences and imagination.

My personal reading has taken me on some magnificent journeys through short stories by Anton Chekhov, Ernest Hemingway, Raymond Carver, Kurt Vonnegut, Richard Ford, Alice Munro, Joyce Carol Oates, et al. I'm drawn to stories that don't easily resolve, but linger instead, offering suggestions … food for thought to be savoured and digested slowly. Over time, they nourish and enhance the events, thoughts, and concerns of my own life.

In my short stories, as in my recent novel, ***Circles of Confusion***, it is my goal to allow you, the reader, some ambiguity as to the outcomes, so we can collaborate as a team; a dialogue of sorts … an intimate conversation that challenges you to question before arriving at a decision. Is that not the way life works?

Some of these stories are humorous, others are dark. Some start as humorous but become dark, and vice versa. That too, is life.

MEMORY TRAIN

"Hello, my name is Jake." The old man introduces himself to the woman when they arrive simultaneously at their seats.

"Do you mind if I sit next to the window?" he asks. "I love watching the world whiz by."

"Not at all," the woman answers.

"What is your name?" Jake asks.

"Sarah," she answers hesitantly.

"Sarah," Jake repeats. "That's a pretty name. It was my wife's name so it should be easy for me to remember yours. My wife passed away a few weeks ago. Her name was Sarah. What is your name?"

The woman remains quiet with a quizzical scrunch to her face. Instead of answering, she places both Jake's and her own carry-on bags on the shelf above their seats.

Jake assumes the window seat and stares toward the outside, watching passengers coming and going on the platform. Porters push baggage around on carts and a desperate mother pulls a crying child by the arm, shouting in a flurry of last-minute anxieties. From inside the train Jake can't hear any of their voices; he can only watch their mouths move and speculates the words by attempting to read their lips. Soon the train lurches and begins to move forward, accompanied by the soft creaking of springs and the grinding of steel wheels against rails. In no time at all, daylight streams through the windows and Jake squints his eyes to adjust.

"I like to imagine that our train is standing still, and the rest of the world is moving past us very fast," Jake observes. "Do you ride the train very often, um …?"

"Sarah," she answers.

"What?"

"Sarah. My name is Sarah."

The old man nods in agreement. "Sarah, yes. I miss her very much. She's been gone a long time you know. I've been living alone since she passed on many years ago."

"I don't ride the train very often."

"What?" Jake asks.

"You asked me if I ride the train often. Not a lot. I usually fly whenever I can."

"I don't like to fly. It scares me; too dangerous. Besides, there are too many terrorists out there these days."

Sarah opens a magazine to read while Jake concentrates on the passing landscape. Without warning, another train zooms by in the opposite direction splattering a stroboscopic repetition of light and dark across Jake's vision. He closes his eyes to avoid dizziness.

"I've ridden a lot of trains in my life. Yes indeed, a lot of trains; different kinds of trains, mind you. Did you know that there are many different kinds of trains?"

Sarah continues reading her magazine.

"Yes," Jake continues. "Many kinds: fast trains, slow trains, loud trains and quiet ones; there are even good trains and evil trains."

Jake closes his eyes and is soon transported to another time.

* * *

We have just made such wonderful love together. Our naked bodies stretch out facing the ceiling staring upward at the ornate plaster detailing in the honeymoon suite of the Mount Royal Hotel.

Sarah starts to laugh. "Just take a look at the size of this bed, my darling. It's so massive, and we made love on every square inch of it. It's such a mess, isn't it?"

I join her in laughter. "This is the largest bed we'll ever make love in,

I'm sure of that. The mess, however, is not for us to worry about. They have housekeepers who make the beds here."

Sarah turns toward me and strokes her fingers across my chest. "Will you promise to bring us here so we can make love in this bed on our 25th and on our 50th anniversaries? Write down the room number so we won't forget."

I tap my hands against my bare chest. "I'm sorry, I don't have my fountain pen with me at this moment," I laugh.

Sarah laughs even harder, struggling to get the next words out of her mouth. "How will we ever manage on the train? How can we make love in those tiny little bunk beds?"

We turn to each other, throw all the covers and blankets aside, and make extra love to make up for the night we will have to spend in bunk beds on the train to Halifax.

In the morning, Sarah is stunningly beautiful sitting across the breakfast table from me. She fusses with her silk napkin and appears to avoid looking into my eyes, but when she finally looks up, her eyelashes flutter to tease me, and her smiling red lips return me to last night in the hotel room where we travelled to places I could never have imagined.

The hotel dining room is busy, mainly with commercial travellers in a rush to meet schedules and appointments. For Sarah and me, the only appointment to consider now is to arrive at track seven in time for the departure, and I've already arranged for the Red Caps to take our luggage down. We can finally relax. For now, I just want to gaze into Sarah's dark alluring eyes and watch her beautiful lips undulate as she chews, talks and smiles; I only hope she never loses her smile.

The waiter arrives with a vase of fresh flowers. "Special roses for the newlyweds, courtesy of the hotel management. Does Madame wish some fresh café?" he asks Sarah. She smiles her acknowledgement to the waiter, but it's a different smile than she reveals to me, a public smile. "And café for Monsieur as well?"

"Oui, s'il vous plait," I respond.

* * *

"Where am I now?" Jake asks, rubbing his eyes following a lengthy sleep.

"Somewhere around Sudbury, I think," Sarah responds, "although I haven't been paying too much attention."

"What am I doing in Sudbury? I want to go home. This isn't my home. Sarah! Where's my Sarah?"

"I'm here."

"I want to see *my* Sarah. She looks after me."

At Sarah's request, an attendant arrives to console Jake until he manages to return to sleep.

* * *

The train to Halifax is long and equipped with Pullman dining cars, sleepers, and many coaches. From our coach window we can watch both the front and the rear of the train while it maneuvers a long curve. As dusk draws near, fog rolls across the St. Lawrence, spreading a soft magenta blanket over the narrow seigneurial farm fields. Sarah and I hold our hands together and gaze at the magic unfolding outside our window, while quietly pondering, each in our own mind, the magic of our future life together. More immediate, however, are the thoughts of sleeping the second night of our honeymoon in bunk beds on a moving train. A Red Cap arrives to rearrange our seating into beds and to explain their practical use. Of course, Sarah and I are not particularly interested in the practical usage, but how impractical the romantic usage will prove to be.

In true chivalry, I assume the upper berth and relinquish the lower to Sarah. I kiss her goodnight and, for a fleeting moment, sense the warmth and contours of her body close to mine before we separate for the night. Once settled into my upper cubicle I experience difficulty in organizing my body to fit, and I can hear Sarah tossing about beneath me.

"I love you Jacob," she whispers.

"I love you too, Sarah, with all my heart. Goodnight."

The rolling of the cars and the grating of the wheels become normal after a while, almost so they can be ignored. What cannot be ignored is the infernal snoring from a berth further along the corridor.

"Are you asleep, Jacob?" Sarah whispers.

"No. I can't sleep."

"Neither can I. Come down here and join me. I'll make some room for you."

I descend from my upper berth to the open sheets of Sarah's bed. Anticipation prepares us both for immediate contact and prolonged pleasure. There is something incredibly sensual about the sounds, vibrations, and rocking movements of a train in the night when two people in love are conjoined in such restrictive quarters.

* * *

Jake awakens and gazes into the ebony blackness of Northern Ontario, as if nothing at all exists outside the windows of his VIA capsule. Does anything exist outside of Jake?

A woman who appears to be vaguely familiar is asleep on the seat next to him. Elsewhere in the car, others are sleeping. Those still awake are reading by small, focused lamps. Jake doesn't recognize anyone. There's a soft mist obscuring the connection between his vision and his cognition, a blurring of facts that come and go without warning. Could the woman sleeping across the aisle be his mother, or his sister? What about the bearded man three seats ahead, could it be his father, the one who disappeared from the family home when Jake was a very young lad, or a distant uncle, perhaps even a Rabbi from his youth? When he looks into the window he sees nothing except an unfamiliar face staring back at him from outside. He jumps back, fear written across his face.

'Who is that man? I've seen him somewhere before. Why is he following me?'

* * *

"Rebecca, don't bother your father," Sarah warns. "He's reading some important papers from the office. Come sit with me, over here."

"It's not a problem, Sarah. Let the girl be," I tell her.

"But you told me not to let the children bother you during the trip. You said that you must finish the litigation papers before we arrive in Toronto, and we're already past Kingston."

"I know what I said, but children must be children. We mustn't try to make them into adults before their time."

"Where is Micah?" Sarah probes.

Rebecca points down the aisle. "He went that way."

"Come Rebecca," Sarah beckons. "We'll find your brother and leave papa alone with his work."

I promise to meet them in the dining car in about an hour. "By then I'll be finished with this." I slap the paper with the back of my hand. "This," I repeat. "This atrocious document of injustice."

The train slows to a stop and several passengers prepare to disembark. I peer out the window to read, Belleville, on the sign overhanging the station front.

'How can they do this to me?' I demand. I've worked hard, every day of my life, and now, they want to take everything away from me: my house, my business, even my car. Next they'll want my children and my wife.' I become inwardly silent, staring out the window at the passengers and the railway workers. My own reflection stares back.

"Keep your jobs," I shout to the workers outside, but my window shields them from hearing my advice. "Whatever you do, don't go into business for yourself. They'll hang you from the rafters, those bastards. There's always somebody out there to get you."

An attendant approaches. He places his hand on my shoulder and asks if everything is all right.

"No, nothing is all right." I want to rant but realize the attendant can't ease my situation. I slouch over, placing my head into my hands.

"Would a coffee or tea help sir?"

"Tea. Yes, a tea might help. Thank you."

* * *

The mist in Jake's mind dissipates as he recognizes the reflection in the window as his own and he's relieved. The woman remains sleeping next to him, but he now recognizes her as the nice woman who helped him earlier with his luggage. 'What was her name? I don't remember. I must ask her when she wakes up.'

Outside in the first light of dawn, a sign declares Thunder Bay as the train slows to a crawl. The woman next to him opens her eyes.

"Where are we?" she asks. Jake points to the sign.

Sarah suggests that they proceed down the aisle to the dining car where they can get some breakfast. She helps Jake up from his seat and offers to let him lead the way, but his chivalry insists that she walk ahead. They arrive at the dining car and are seated at a table.

* * *

I finish my tea just as the train starts moving away from Belleville. Upon checking my watch, I remember that Sarah and the children are waiting for me in the dining car.

"You're late, Jacob. We've been sitting here for more than an hour. What have you been doing? The children are getting hungry, and you know that makes them irritable."

"I've been going through the papers, over and over. There is nothing more we can do to stop them. It's all over, Sarah. Finished. Kaput!"

"Not now, Jacob. Not in front of the children."

"When would you like to discuss this, Sarah, before or after some other family lives in our house? Already you can't drive your Mercedes; you don't own it anymore. The bastards have taken everything."

"Please, Jacob. Don't use that language in front of the children."

"Here are the facts. We're riding in the train because we no longer have our cars. When we arrive in Toronto, we'll move into the house of your sister, probably in a basement apartment or in the attic. We'll take public transit wherever we go, and the children will attend public school from now on; no more private this and private that, no more piano and violin lessons, no more fund-raising boards of governors, no more furs and thousand-dollar purses. We'll both look for suitable employment. In short, we'll

become like normal people; the kinds of people I just watched working at the train station, pushing carts around and selling tickets. Maybe I could get one of those jobs. Maybe you could."

* * *

Before it enters the prairies, the VIA train surges through the final leg of Northern Ontario. Kenora is behind them now with Winnipeg the next stop, less than an hour away.

Jake remains quiet, watching the forest gradually cede to flatter, more agricultural terrain. At one time, Winnipeg was the hub of Canada's rail system. Every shipment passed through the city whether pointed east or west, and it was the end of the road for livestock.

As Jake watches the new landscape unfold, he also witnesses row upon row of empty cattle cars waiting on sidings for their next assignments.

* * *

"Jacob. Stay away from the door," my grandfather warns. "You don't want anybody to see you. We have to be careful."

I question him. "Why did mama and us children come to live with you, Zayda? What was wrong with the other house? Why has papa left us to live on our own here? Where did he go?"

"There are too many questions for such a young boy, Jacob" my grandfather offers. "There are even too many questions for us old people to understand these days."

It's the hard determined knocking against the solid oak front door that sends chills through all of us, young and old alike.

"Open the door!" a voice demands. We and mama run toward the back rooms to hide in a closet while Zayda opens the door, but there is no place to hide. The soldiers push Zayda to the floor and begin rummaging through each and every room, smashing and tearing at furniture and bedding. We're rounded up and ordered to leave the house. Outside, there are others like us rounded up, while clumps of neighbours stand in their

doorsteps and stare. Anyone who resists is beaten; in some cases, they are shot on the spot. Our family's belongings are left behind for looters and fortune seekers to pillage.

I ask, "What will happen to all the beautiful paintings, Zayda … the Renoirs and the Monets? Can we take them with us?"

As I'm led away, I see my close friend's family watching. I wave at them, but they don't return the gesture. Instead, they turn their sad eyes to the ground.

At the railroad yard, lines of empty cattle cars await their next cargo. Names are called and one by one, the people are pushed into the cars until hundreds of us are stuffed into each one. My sister and I attempt to stay close to mama and her arms reach out to bring us close. Hundreds of people, stuffed tighter than hogs, weeping, coughing, choking, reeking, puking and pissing onto the floor and on each other. There is no place to sit down, only to stand, even after the legs can stand no longer. The train moves on, long rows of cattle cars and their human cargo wend through the countryside to only God knows where.

An old man beside me dies standing up and can't even fall down. His corpse remains pinned between us. He has already shit his pants and the smell permeates everything. Someone attempts to push open the door, but it's padlocked from the outside. Our doom is sealed. Others die from the heat and choke from their own vomit.

* * *

Jake alternates between perceived realities and clouds of confusion, occasionally interrupted by patches where nothing exists. Colours are visualized without form or content, leaving only suggestions for his memory to consider. As they roll into Calgary the train passes a billboard promoting the Calgary Stampede. A cowboy astride a palomino stallion swings his lariat above him in imagined pursuit of a calf.

Between the open fields of golden prairie wheat are wedged sections of yellow canola, all waving east and west in the breeze as the train follows its historical route, the same rails as opened the Canadian West 130 years before. Layered above the yellow and gold, a sheet of solid deep azure sky, wide and open, fills the vista.

The bright yellow canola strikes a chord with Jake.

* * *

As I ride my bicycle home from the railway station, still wearing my ticket-takers uniform, I am ignored by my neighbours as I pass. Pride has been left behind in the years following the collapse of the business. I've since managed to accept one of the truths of life: the Lord giveth and the Lord taketh away. It could have been much worse I suppose. What if I couldn't find work? What if I had ended up begging on the street? What if my mother hadn't pushed me under the cattle car when we arrived at the camp, and what if I hadn't escaped through the farm fields eating only the leftovers in the fields? No thanks! I've done that before. Any job would do and cleaning up around the stationhouse is a good job, at least for the moment. It's respectable, it's legal, and I receive payment for my work.

The humble apartment we moved into after living in my sister-in-law's basement is small, the main floor of an old tenement house, but it offers a moderate level of comfort. We have access to a portion of the backyard where I maintain a modest vegetable garden during the growing season. A patch of afternoon sunlight manages to fall onto the garden between the massive maples on both sides of the yard.

Sarah wants us to move into a larger, fancier place, one of the new high-rise buildings down close to the lake, but of course we would both have to work to manage one of those, and Sarah hasn't yet accepted our new situation, even though her old friends from the library and the art gallery foundations don't call her anymore. Their art gallery luncheons don't match our current income, and Sarah has refused to leave the apartment since we moved there seven years ago.

"Sarah, I'm home," I announce, as I do every evening, realizing that I may not receive a response. Sarah has become very quiet of late; communication between us is limited, but I repeat, "Sarah, I'm home," mainly to hear a voice; any voice.

As usual, I change from my uniform into something more casual before preparing dinner. Upon opening the door to the garden my eyes are attracted to a yellow shape fluttering back and forth in the breeze. Suspended from an outstretched branch of the large maple, Sarah's lifeless form confronts me, a noose placed around her neck and a fallen ladder at her feet. She chose to wear the only hint of colour left in our lives, an old flowery yellow summer dress.

* * *

When the train arrives in Vancouver, Jake's consciousness has fogged over; all knowledge of the present has abandoned him. People rise from their seats to disembark but they don't register with him. They just represent movement, not people, just movement going nowhere. Jake has no destination, no concept of time or space. Sarah takes Jake's arm and leads him through the confusing maze, gathering luggage and looking around the station for a familiar face.

"Over here, Sarah," a large woman in her 50s shouts and waves. Her voice echoes in the vastness of Pacific Central Station. "We're over here."

"Hi Mom. What a long trip. We're so tired. I don't think Grandpa is feeling too well though. He hasn't uttered two words since Winnipeg. It's almost like he's in some kind of a trance or something."

"He's just tired Sarah, that's all." The woman turns to Jake and gives him a hug. "Oh Dad. It's so good to see you again. How was the train ride? You always liked travelling by train, didn't you?"

"I want to go home. I'm ready to go home now."

"You are home, Dad. You've made the right decision by coming out here, that's for sure. The whole family lives out here now. We've arranged for a room in a wonderful home for you; you'll be able to see the ocean from your window. How does that sound? They'll look after you there, don't you worry a bit. We'll come to visit you often."

LESSONS LEARNED

FULL COUNT

Hamilton, 1956:

"Hey, you … new kid!" a voice calls to me from across the school hallway. "What's your name?"

"Who, me?" I answer. "I'm Eddy. I just arrived here to start grade eight. What's your name?"

"Just call me Larry, 'cause that's my name, eh?" He laughs toward some other kids. They join his laughter.

I wave, "Hi guys."

"I'll tell you what," Larry says. "Me and my buddies are heading out tomorrow night to have some fun. You can join us if you want. Meet us at the top of the Jolley Cut after supper."

I don't know any other kids at the school, so I agree to meet with Larry and his friends the next evening.

As instructed, I arrive at the corner of Concession Street near the Jolley Cut, a location that offers a panoramic view from the top of Hamilton Mountain to the city centre below. Darkness is descending. A seemingly abandoned vine-covered Victorian house, resembling every haunted house I had ever seen in the movies, occupies the corner.

Whispering voices, buzzing like a colony of honey bees, emanate from the garden beside the house. Amid the drone, Larry's voice whispers, "Psst, Eddy. Over here."

I follow the voice, prying my way through a tangled jungle of overgrown grapevines until I arrive at a small clearing where my new friends are sitting.

"Here, try this," Larry offers, passing me a cigarette. He appears to be the undisputed leader of the group. Not wanting to be excluded, I accept, inhale a reluctant puff and fold into a coughing fit, while the others, following Larry's lead, laugh in unison.

"Okay, Eddy, here's the scoop," Larry says. "Eat as many of these grapes as you can, then we'll take you to our secret cave."

It all sounds so mysterious to me, but I nod my head in agreement when Larry asks if I'm in with them.

I claw my way among the vines, picking and gobbling the sweet purple grapes.

From the shroud of darkness, a firm hand grips my arm. Turning, I'm face-to-face with the silhouette of a large figure, that of a wizened old man, pinned against the weak glow of window light.

"What the hell are you doing on my property?" the silhouette demands in a gruff voice. He shakes my arm harshly until the grapes squash in my hand. The coolness of the fresh juice flows between my tightened fingers.

I scream.

Larry and the other boys escape to the open street laughing all the way. The silhouette loosens his grasp. I seize the opportunity to join my new buddies, leaving the old man alone in his vineyard.

Once the thrill of stealing grapes and of escaping certain death wears off, we turn our attention to trekking down a trail along the steep edge of the escarpment. Larry starts singing some dirty words about someone called Sally who's riding on a pony (to the melody of Yankee Doodle) and challenges the rest of us to create our own bawdy lyrics.

We each carry a stick to assist us on the trail and smash away at weeds and rocks as we walk. Several of the boys engage me in a mock sword fight, challenging me to maintain balance on the narrow trail.

We arrive at an opening in the mountainside; I assume it's the secret cave Larry was talking about. Cigarette butts, beer cans, and used condoms litter the shale floor, evidence that others share the secret of the cave. From the cave's entrance, the city lights below shimmer like a forest of flickering Christmas trees. Without warning, Stelco's ovens bellow balls of fire and smoke into the northern sky. In only minutes, the temperature increases against my skin.

Larry lights a candle that casts eerie shadows against the cavern walls. We compete with creative hand shadows in an attempt to illustrate Sally Doodle's pony ride.

"Speaking of Sally," Larry begins. "You all know Sally, eh? The chick in our class who sits at the back of the room; the one with the tight sweaters. Everybody knows Sally, eh?" Larry cups his hands in front of his chest to describe her. "She's a real class honey. I actually got it on with her in the boiler room of the school," he boasts. "You know, down where all the water pipes are." He describes the location and the act in vivid detail. "We had just finished up when old Jimmy, the janitor, came in. He almost caught us in the act."

None of us utter a word. Larry continues, "I can arrange for any of you guys to have her too ... for a price of course ... if you're not too chicken shit, that is." Nobody volunteers.

Suddenly, I'm overcome with the onset of an urgent bowel movement. Larry bursts into laughter, and the boys join him. "It's those damned Concord grapes you were eating, Eddy. Get the hell outside, you're not shitting in here. And don't try to shit uphill, either; it's messier than pissing into the wind. Ha-ha."

In the dark, I trip over a tree root while attempting to pull up my jeans and tumble a few yards down the slope before settling on a small ledge. No bones are broken but I suffer from a sore knee and a rip in my jeans, not to mention the embarrassment at being caught with my pants around my ankles. The boys, still laughing, form a human chain to rescue me.

It finally occurs to me that the only reason I'm invited is to be the brunt of their humour.

On our return up the escarpment, a mist rolls in over the brow.

When we arrive at the parking lot for Mount Hamilton General Hospital, the mist becomes a dense fog.

"You guys know what to do, Larry says. "Eddy, you come with me."

The other boys spread out across the parking lot disappearing into the fog. Larry hands me a screwdriver. "See how many wheel covers you can rip off these cars before getting caught. Concentrate on the ones with spinners. They work the best."

"Why?" I ask, "What are we going to do with them?"

"Nothing," Larry answers. "We'll just toss them over the mountain and watch how far they go."

"That sounds pretty stupid to me," I offer.

"Are you calling me stupid?" Larry asks, clutching the collar of my shirt in his fist. "Just do what the fuck I tell you, you dumb-ass prick."

"What happens if I get caught?"

"Tough shit. You're on your own, and if you rat on me, I'll tear your balls apart."

As soon as I'm separated from Larry in the fog, I skip for home.

For a few weeks I suffer name-calling and discomfort from Larry and his followers, but I soon encounter new friends who share my interests in sports and music. Fortunately for me, but unfortunate for them, there are other class members for Larry to prey on.

* * *

When my name is called during the eighth grade graduation ceremony, I'm the only male among my female classmates to receive honours. My short-lived buddies from Larry's gang harass me with whistles and hisses from the back row. The word 'suckhole' rings dominant among several other phrases.

During my summer vacation between elementary and high school, I join the baseball league at Inch Park. It's real hardball, not just wimpy softball like we play at school. In addition to being a first-string pitcher for the Panthers, I'm also an above average hitter.

To hit well means that you can't be afraid to swing at the ball.

There's no reward for being timid when there's a chance you could connect. You must take risks; all the big-time sluggers take risks.

It's the bottom of the ninth, two runners on base, two out, the count is three and two against me — full count — a true-life Casey At The Bat, the defining moment for my baseball career. What will I be, a hero or a loser?

Like a missile, a fastball hones in on me. With less than ten feet between me and the ball, I begin my swing from high above my right shoulder. Experience dictates the precise moment of my release and will determine the moment of impact.

The night is still; everyone's eyes are fixed. Even the mosquitoes surrounding the infield lights seem frozen. Players, coaches, girl-friends, brothers, mothers and fathers, wait for the connection, the crack of the bat that will drive the ball far beyond the reach of the outfielders, at least far enough to allow two runners in. We're only down one run, so I won't even have to make it around the bags. I just have to belt it far enough for a double.

The whoosh of hardwood cutting through air, followed by the firm finality of hard ball against leather catcher's mitt, are the last sounds of the game that matter to me. I don't hear the umpire shout, "Ste-e-rike three, you're out," nor do the jubilant cheers of the opposing team and its fans reach me; the bitching of my own teammates remain mute. I quietly hang my mitt over the handlebars of my red CCM and point it toward the drug store soda shop where I hope to drown my sorrows in a cherry coke.

I sit alone in a booth designed for four. The only other people in the shop are Larry and Sally, who are doubled over a two-straw chocolate shake in the next booth. Larry turns to me over the back of the booth, whispering, "Hey, what's up Eddy? Remember what I told you, eh? I can set you and Sally up for a roll in the sack if you wanna. Just say the word." Larry hides his words from Sally by shielding his mouth with the back of his hand.

My eyes connect with Sally's across the table. We stare without blinking; smiles appear simultaneously on our lips. I coolly ease my own hand-protected mouth close to Larry's ear, my eyes firmly fixed on Sally's. "Screw off asshole," I assert, returning to my cherry coke.

* * *

I manage to complete my sojourn at high school. Others are not so blessed. Sally, whom I've never been closer to than in Larry's imagination, becomes pregnant in her second year and gives birth to a baby boy who, in later years, will bear an uncanny resemblance to her math teacher.

Other boys from the gang, suffering from the effects of Larry's leadership, fall into a range of illicit pursuits: possession of stolen goods, drug dealing, human trafficking, and assault. Year after year, the newspapers repeat their names and the length of their sentences.

The boy on my baseball team who eagerly waited at second base for the hit that would allow him to slide into home for the winning run — the hit that never came — steers his rusted 1948 Dodge convertible around the hairpin at Albion Falls following a class party. He's last seen alive dropping out of the airborne convertible, skidding across the pavement on his ass, and flinging over the escarpment.

* * *

Years later, while anxiously awaiting the results of my X-rays, I ponder. What decides our lot in life? What are the odds? Is it an accumulation of all the decisions we make, from day-to-day, hour-to-hour, or is it merely a luck of the draw, choosing the correct ace in the deck?

Would my life be different if I'd stolen one of those wheel covers and flung it over the escarpment? What if I'd had sex with Sally? She was a turn-on after all. What if I hadn't taken that first cigarette from Larry? Maybe then things would be different. We'll never know.

"Hello, Eddy? I'm Doctor Lewiston. Have a seat."

"Larry? Larry Lewiston?"

Lessons learned.

THE SHRINKING MAN

Summer 1957:

My first 15 years of life have been a tightly scheduled ritual of attending school, playing baseball, and practising the piano, but for two weeks each summer, our family vacations at a rustic lodge in Southampton, Ontario.

When we arrive, it's the smell of the lodge that I remember from previous years, a permeation of wood smoke combined with cedar and mustiness, overcorrected with a hint of lavender soap and scented towels.

We have always shared the same room, but this year, I'm given a separate bedroom, attached to my parent's room through a common bath. They told me it's because of my age, that I'm finally old enough to have my own private room, but I know better. Mom and Dad want to be alone this year, not a thought that I'm comfortable with. Think of it. Mom and Dad? Ugh!

"Does everyone know what day it is?" Mom challenges. She assumes the role of tour director, not only during our summer vacations, but for everything else in our lives as well. On the first Friday evening of our holiday, it's a tradition for us to join the other lodgers on a sunset cruise that motors out into Lake Huron, past the lighthouse, and around Chantry Island.

"Do I have to go on that dumb boat?" I complain. "Why do we always do the same thing, year after year? I hate that boat. There's nobody to talk to, just a bunch of old people, that's all."

"Of course, we must," Mom counters. "It's a tradition. Besides, it's only one evening of boredom out of the entire year."

"My whole life is boring. Nothing ever changes."

* * *

Seated alone at the stern, I stare into the spray that boils to the surface of the water as the yacht circles Chantry Island. The muffled rumble of the inboard blends with the mumbling drone of adult conversation.

My attention is diverted to a pair of newlyweds gazing romantically at the setting sun from the starboard. They're spending their honeymoon at the lodge and, like me, are oblivious to the other conversations on board.

I can't ignore the bride's well-tanned and oiled skin glowing in the final golden moments of the sunset and how her tapered legs fit snugly against the cuffs of her white form-fitting shorts. I watch, with keen interest, as the groom tenderly walks his fingers, yellow-page style, tickling the surface of her bared midriff. She giggles and shifts her torso. He responds by drawing her closer. She stares into his eyes and teases his lips with the tip of her tongue. They kiss.

A moment into the kiss the bride catches me leering. She teasingly winks and blows a kiss toward me, forcing me to divert my attention elsewhere. Searching randomly about the yacht for a new subject, my eyes settle on a girl sporting a naval motif dickey, a dime-store admiral's cap, and white bobby socks. She too, had been watching the newlyweds and smiles toward me in shared appreciation. Her smile reveals a mouthful of silver braces, reflecting the final rays of the setting sun. To avoid her stare, I return my attention to the water spraying up from the stern.

When the yacht returns to port we all disembark only to reassemble at the lodge for drinks and socializing.

"Please excuse us," the groom pleads. "We're terribly exhausted. It must be the fresh air," he explains politely as he and his new bride retire to their room.

A red-faced man, with nicotine stains on his fingers, snickers to his cronies and offers an aside, nudging his elbow into his buddy's chest. "Fresh air my arse," he says loudly. "They're not as exhausted as they're going to be. Har-har."

"Alf, that's not very nice," nags the man's wife, "especially in front of the young boy." Her head nods in my direction.

My concentration is focused on the groom's hand while it caresses his bride's lower back as the couple ascend the staircase to their room. The dickey-clad girl focuses directly on my fascination with the lovebirds, a fascination that clings to my imagination well into the night.

* * *

In the morning following breakfast, a new growth of pimples stare back at me from the mirror in the bathroom.

"I hate these things. How can I get rid of them?"

"Just leave them alone," my mother orders. "They'll disappear. It's just a stage you're going through. Whatever you do, don't pick them. They'll become permanent if you do. You don't want to end up with a face like Uncle Harold's, do you?"

I squeeze one of the whiteheads until it bursts. "I'm bored. There's nothing to do here. Why can't we go home?"

* * *

Changing into my bathing suit, I grab a towel and start toward the grand expanse of Southampton's sandy beach.

"If you're going to the beach, put some lotion on before you go out," Mom orders another edict. "Otherwise you'll burn to a crisp," she warns, like she always does.

I ignore her.

I have the beach to myself. The sun sits high overhead, there's not a cloud in sight, and the sand is already hot under my tender feet. After a casual swim, I return to the sand, dry myself, and lay down on my towel, exposing my pale white chest and legs to the sun. A soft breeze rolls over me. Hypnotized by the steady drone of the rolling surf, the events of the previous night echo in my head like a Duane Eddy reverb. I ponder whether the newlyweds might have sensed my illusory participation in their intimacies. An emerging discomfort leads me further into my private world where the outcome is yet unknown.

Suddenly, my solitary space is invaded. A shadow casts over me, selectively cooling my burning chest.

"Hi there. Do you mind if I put my towel down here?" a giggly voice inquires.

I strain my neck to look toward the voice. Silhouetted between my eyes and the bright sun stands a shapely girl in a two-piece bathing suit. A fleeting thought suggests that I may still be dreaming but tighter squinting reveals the dickey-clad girl from the yacht who appears much older without the dickey and naval cap.

I hesitate before mustering enough courage to speak. "Um ... sure ... that's okay ... sure, it's a public beach after all."

She peers directly into my squinting eyes. "I'm Virginia," she giggles without any delay. "What's your name?"

I'm unnerved by her directness. "Eddy, I answer."

"Where're you from, Eddy?" she probes, snapping her brace-covered teeth into a wad of bubble gum.

"Hamilton. I'm from Hamilton."

"I was there two years ago to visit my aunt. She lives up on the mountain. It's too big a city for me. I'd get lost there." She giggles again.

Stars sparkle from her silver braces. I wonder what it might be like to kiss someone with braces on her teeth. Would my tongue catch on the barbs?

She continues to ramble. "I saw you last night on the boat. It's really boring but I have to be there every Friday. My dad's the captain and he forces me to dress up in that stupid costume. He says the tourists really like it, but I don't think they care at all."

I muster enough courage to ask, "So you live here all year long?"

"Yeah, I'm afraid so. Right there." She blows a bubble and points to a house partially hidden from public view by a hedge. "It's really pretty boring, especially during the winter."

Virginia places her towel at a respectable distance from mine. She rubs lotion over her exposed skin before lying down on her back. I attempt to appear disinterested by gazing off toward some seagulls. A period of silence prevails until she rolls over onto her stomach, bracing her head with her right arm. Her face points toward mine.

"Would you mind rubbing some of that lotion on my back?" she asks. "I can't reach it by myself."

I want to say something cool and confident like, "Anytime, gorgeous," as Bogart would say in the movies, but I can only manage, "Okay," as if it were a chore. I gingerly daub the cream, barely touching her skin.

"You should turn over from time to time," she warns me. "You're going to get burned to a crisp."

"You sound just like my mother," I tell her before turning onto my stomach in obeyance.

"You don't get much sun, do you?" Virginia observes, nodding toward my city-white back. "You should really use something to protect yourself. Here, let me rub some of this on you."

Before I have a chance to answer, a chill consumes my entire body as she passes her soft lotion-covered fingers across my pale back and legs. I'm already unnerved about the bold directness of her stare whenever she talks to me but am disappointedly relieved when she stops massaging at the top edge of my bathing suit.

I want to move closer to her but my shyness and fear of the unknown causes me to resist. Virginia isn't shy. She stands up, shakes some sand from her towel, and repositions it adjacent to mine. I wonder if she can read my mind.

Now closer, our conversation becomes more relaxed and personal. Virginia takes the lead. We discuss music, ice cream flavours, and school courses. Virginia reveals that she's sixteen, a full year older than me, a fact that creates a further level of anxiety for me. I lie to her, "Me too."

"How about that couple on the boat last night, eh?" Virginia laughs, snapping her gum. "Did you see her egg him on when he rubbed her ass? I'd have given anything to be a fly on their wall last night, wouldn't you? Whew!"

"No kidding," I chuckle nervously, but am titillated by her boldness.

Following a prolonged period of silence, Virginia leans forward, narrowing the gap between our faces; so close I can smell her Bazooka bubble gum.

"I have a great idea," she says. "Take me to the movies tonight. They're showing 'The Incredible Shrinking Man.' I'll meet you in front of The Esquire at seven."

I hesitate before agreeing. "Sure ... OK."

She lifts herself, flicks the sand from her towel, and disappears down the boardwalk.

* * *

Following supper, I wash up and change into my best clothes, taking extra care in brushing my teeth and combing my hair. I daub Clearasil on my new outcrop of pimples and finally, to look older, I tousle the front of my hair, like Elvis.

I lie to my parents. "I met some guys on the beach and we're going to the show. It's some horror show," I emphasize, just to guarantee they don't show up at the movies as well. Briefly, I consider the possibility that they might welcome an evening by themselves. 'Ugh!'

I wait nervously on the sidewalk under the Esquire marquee. Virginia appears moments later across the street. Her hair, hanging loosely, seems longer, and it bounces freely with the rhythm of her steps as she slowly crosses the street with the determination of a fashion model on a catwalk. Her eyes focus directly into mine. I watch her cotton print dress flare outward from her slender waist, as it responds to the rise and fall of her hips.

"Hi Eddy!" Virginia greets with a confident, musical voice as if we've known each other for years. When she smiles and looks firmly into my eyes, I'm stricken by her mascara and glossy red lipstick.

I have just enough money to cover our admission and one bag of buttered popcorn. I give the popcorn to Virginia.

She leads the way through the curtain and into the dimness of the theatre, immediately choosing seats in the back row. While entering the row from the aisle, my hand accidentally connects with the tight elasticized waist of her dress that lowers into her back's subtle curvature, the same curve I noticed earlier on the beach. My heart rate increases while recalling last night's vision of the bridegroom's hands wandering on his new bride's back.

We're seated for only a moment before the lights dim and the screen comes to life with a cartoon and previews of future films. When 'The Incredible Shrinking Man' begins, light flickering from the screen profiles Virginia's face against the darkness; she looks like a beautiful movie star.

We sit quietly for some time staring at the screen.

Virginia breaks the ice. "Do you want some popcorn?" she whispers. Before I can respond, she feeds a popcorn ball between my lips with her fingers. I taste the salt and butter on her fingertips.

"Tastes good, eh? Here, have another one." She feeds me again. Once again, I savour the salt on her fingers as they penetrate my lips. Her sharp fingernail pricks against my tongue.

"This is going to be a scary movie." Virginia whispers airily into my ear. "I love scary movies, but they make me really nervous. I'll feel safer if you put your arm around my shoulder." She leans toward me.

After a moment of hesitation, I oblige. Virginia reacts by leaning her head on my shoulder. Her soft curls tickle the skin on my neck and my entire body fills with magic. Attempting to sneak a look at her screen-lit profile once again, I encounter her gazing straight into my eyes. She stares without blinking for what seems an eternity. Her lips open into an inviting smile, and her braces twinkle against the darkness. Fate moves us closer together until our lips touch. Her lips are soft and moist. I gaze into her eyes until her lids slowly close; I reciprocate, entranced by her willingness. I want the kiss to last forever.

We're drawn together like opposite poles of a magnet, vulnerable to every sigh and shiver, every flickering eyelid and quivering whisper. I feel Virginia's tongue parting my lips. She flutters the end of her tongue against mine. Like pioneers in a strange land, we explore further into the unknown. I taste the sweetness of Virginia's lipstick. My earlier fascination is satisfied when my tongue slips between the metallic hardness of her braces and the soft inner surface of her upper lip. My body quivers.

Our spell is broken abruptly by the appearance of a giant spider attacking the shrinking man on the screen. Virginia, whose eyes snap open in response to the abrupt change in the music, jumps in her seat. "Oh, my God!"

She places one hand over her mouth to prevent a scream, then re-closes her eyes and forces her face into the dark security of my pounding chest. Amidst the scurry, her right hand grabs the first object in its path.

I panic when her hand grips high on my upper leg, her fingers digging and squeezing against the soft area of my thigh. I respond, expanding rapidly. She softens her grip as a first response to this new revelation, pauses, then returns her curious fingers.

The movie continues without us. Neither cares whether the giant spider eats the shrinking man alive or not. Virginia leans forward and stares into my eyes, moving closer and closer, eager for further responses, something, anything, that will contribute to our expanding repertoire of experiences. Unsure of what should follow, our lips melt into each other's. Virginia gracefully retracts her hand, denying me of a natural resolution.

When the house lights turn on, we exit the theatre to a warm soft evening rain. We wrap our arms around each other like lovers in a movie and stroll along the beach in search of whatever might happen next. The clouds suddenly open to a downpour; we're forced onto the porch surrounding Virginia's family home where we share each other's embraces once again.

Her father's voice passes through the screen door from inside. "Virginia, isn't it about time you called it a night? It's past eleven."

Before I leave, we stop at the edge of the boardwalk, and kiss one last time. It's a short peck of a kiss, nothing like the ones that preceded it. She thanks me for a wonderful evening and promises to see me again.

Awkwardly I thank her as well.

She says, "I have to work for my dad next week, but I can be free on Wednesday. In the meantime, don't forget about me." As a further reminder she presses against me, places her lips on mine and flutters her tongue briefly between my lips, before withdrawing it. "I love you, Eddy," she whispers, adding, "I can hardly wait 'til Wednesday. Sweet dreams."

The remainder of my night is long, sleepless, and painful. Both mind and body refuse to detach themselves from the evening's events; they replay in sequence many times, tossing me between ecstasy and reality. A warm goodness shimmers inside and I suddenly become much older.

* * *

The days that follow are difficult. I yearn desperately to see Virginia again. My impatience for Wednesday's arrival makes the other days extremely long and monotonous. By Tuesday afternoon the anxiety is so unbearable that I walk along the beach toward her house with hopes of capturing a glimpse of her.

As I approach her home, the strains of Jerry Lee Lewis screaming, 'A Whole Lot of Shakin' Going On,' thunder from the radio of a customized, candy-apple red, 1952 Chevy parked in the driveway. In the backyard behind the hedge, a couple shares kisses. An Elvis look-a-like gropes under the girl's blouse and she giggles, teasing him to explore further by seductively loosening a button.

"Virginia?" I ask before thinking.

The couple jumps apart. Virginia attempts to adjust her blouse. Elvis pulls a comb through his hair and walks toward the Chevy.

"Oh … Hi Eddy." She's uncharacteristically short of words. "Um … this is Jimmy." She points in Elvis' direction. "We go to school together. We're in the same class."

"No kidding," I mutter before turning back toward the beach.

"Are we still good for tomorrow?" Virginia calls. "I'll let you take me to the movies."

Fat chance, I mutter to myself.

Lessons learned.

TOUGH GUY

"Just wait until your father comes home," she faced me, pointing her right forefinger at my nose. It was Mom's signal that she needed backup. When Dad arrived home, he was greeted with her pronouncement, "You take care of this. I can't handle him anymore," before she retreated to the neutral corner of the room, leaving my father to figure out what I had done.

I was a mild-mannered, usually friendly kid who, in most circumstances, obeyed the rules of the household and the lessons about how to behave in society as taught to me by my parents. My mother was most directly involved in my upbringing, except when I stepped outside the rules and the crime proved to be more than my mother could handle.

Ultimately, my father would usually agree with her when assigning a punishment. However, between the pronouncement and the punishment, there was a blustering of standard phrases from my father's disciplinary book. My mother maintained a tight-lipped silence from across the room with her arms crossed, a ploy that relinquished some level of empowerment over the situation to my father.

"You did what?" my dad responded; his eyes widened. "We can't have you carrying on like that. What's going through your head, Edward?" They only called me Edward when they were mad at me. The rest of the time I was just Eddy.

It was the response when I tore apart the alarm clock to see how it worked at the age of six, and it was the same response when I stole my father's Buckingham cigarettes at 15. It would always end with Dad ordering, "Now, go to your room while your mother and I discuss this." The discussion would be a short 'raised-voice' back-and-forth battle between my parents that quickly resolved into a calm, but tenuous, agreement. I then knew that the jury had spoken, and Dad would soon deliver the ultimate sentence.

By the time I reached my teens, it became necessary to prove myself to my peers more than to my parents. It was my friends at school who would determine how I should act, what I should wear, what music I should listen to, and what secrets I should keep from my parents. I was introduced to an expanded vocabulary, and certain activities that must surely remain private to within my trusted circle of friends.

It became increasingly important for me to be competitive, not within any sports venues, but in a street-physical way, to demonstrate my ability to survive and to counter the bullying. Survival as a teen became a team sport for me, a balancing act between passive resistance and physical aggression.

The idealism that I had been raised with was one of tolerance. My parents instilled those values in me from early childhood. My idol was Jackie Robinson and I empathized with the trials the baseball icon faced in being accepted into the major leagues as the first professional African-American athlete. I learned to believe strongly in equality for everyone, regardless of their nationality, colour or religion. There were, however, conflicting examples of how that idealism should be achieved.

* * *

In my first year of high school, one of the kids in my class was mouthing racial slurs toward one of my Indigenous friends from the nearby reserve. A flame erupted inside of me that triggered my responsive action. Instinctively, I drove my right fist into the boy's face, an act that fractured his nose. The boy was taken to the hospital and I was led to the principal's office.

"Just wait until your father comes home," my mother warned, in response to the call she received from the school.

"You did what?" my father demanded when he arrived home from work. "We can't have you carrying on like that." He waved his arms in the air. "What's going through your head, Edward?"

I answered my father like never before. "I don't give a shit what you think. The guy had it coming."

Dad's initial reaction was to smack me across the face, but he froze in mid-swipe, his face in a state of disbelief. "Don't you ever use that word in this house." Suddenly Dad became quiet and left my room. The only voice from the living room was my mother's.

"What are we going to do with him? He can't get away with this. He can't solve all his problems with his fists."

My father's voice whispered, "I know, I know ... but I would have done the same thing to the little bastard when I was his age." The jury delivered its sentence after much deliberation and consultation with the principal's office.

Every Wednesday morning, the principal conducted a school-wide meeting in the auditorium. I was ordered to admit to the entire school that I was wrong, that I was sorry for what I had done, and I was directed to publicly shake hands with the injured classmate. My parents arranged the punishment with cooperation from the principal.

On stage, I faced the victim. "I'm really sorry for hitting you." I turned to the assembly. "I also apologize to the entire school for my actions. I was wrong. I should never have used violence; I should have talked to him instead."

Surprisingly, the victim responded by admitting that he was wrong and that he should never have said the things he did in the first place. He apologized to me, to the offended classmate, and to the school. We shook hands. By the end of the term, the victim and I became friends.

Privately, my parents contacted the victim's parents with their apologies and offered to pay their medical expenses but were turned down. "Lessons learned all the way around," is how the victim's father responded.

* * *

In 1965, I was invited through a church affiliation, to travel with a busload of Canadians to Alabama, where we would join the march from Selma to Montgomery with Martin Luther King. I was working in a factory at the time. When I approached my boss to request a week off, the boss replied, "If you want to go and march with a bunch of N…'s then go, but don't come back. You won't have a job."

Sadly, I opted to keep my job, a decision I would regret for the remainder of my life. Ironically, I left the factory three months later to pursue other interests.

* * *

Three years later, when I was in my mid-20's, and working in an office, I attended a trade seminar in Toronto with several of my office mates. At the end of the seminar, my boss asked where we might get a good meal and see some entertainment. As a fanatic jazz fan, I immediately suggested the Colonial Tavern on Yonge Street. The only table available was situated on the mezzanine overlooking the bandstand. There was access to the stage via a stairwell from the mezzanine and several band rooms were situated near our table. The iconic Earl 'Fatha' Hines and his trio was the featured band.

While we were eating, the trio emerged from one of the band rooms. There were tears in 'Fatha' Hines' eyes. He instructed the other two musicians to remain on the mezzanine. "I'm doing this alone," he said to them before walking slowly down the stairs to the stage. I invited the bassist and drummer to sit at our table until they were called down.

"What's going on?" I asked the musicians. "Fatha Hines looked like he was crying."

The bassist answered with tears in his own eyes. "Didn't you hear the news? Dr. King was just assassinated today in Memphis."

Like Jackie Robinson, Martin Luther King had become another of my idols. My eyes swelled, forcing tears to flow down my face. One of my coworkers across the table uttered, "Well, I guess he had it coming, after stirring up all of them N…'s."

Without a thought, I plunged across the table, grabbing the co-worker by his shirt collar. "You son of a bitch," I cursed. My sudden torrent of anger might have thrown the man over the railing were it not for the bassist sitting next to me.

"Hey Brother," the musician said, placing his arm on my shoulder. "I know where you're coming from, man, believe me, I know, but that's not what Dr. King would want you to do. I think you already know that, man."

From the piano, the 'Fatha' announced the passing of Dr. King and began singing with a breaking voice, "Please don't talk about me when I'm gone …"

Lessons learned.

THE LECTURE

"Hello, is this Eddy?" the voice asked on the telephone.

"Yes, this is Eddy."

"Hi. I'm Jacquie from the Dean's office at the college. We're looking for a substitute teacher for a course in Art History. You've been strongly recommended by the current teacher, who will be away on a medical leave. Would you be able to teach part time for the next four weeks? There will be two sections of three hours for a total of six hours per week."

"Hmm ..." I scratched my chin. "I could be."

"Well, we have to make a decision within the next two days. Would that be possible? In the meantime, you could contact the current teacher to discuss the details."

"Thank you Jacquie. I'll do that and let you know by Thursday."

"That would be wonderful. We'll talk to you soon."

Before accepting the assignment I arranged to meet the teacher and attend one of his classes. I sat in the back row and quietly observed the lecture.

The students of the course were technology students (auto mechanics, machine shop, millwrights, etc.) who were required to take the history of art as their liberal arts elective, although there was nothing 'elective' about it. Many, if not all, of the students were being sponsored to attend the college through employment retraining grants. They were being graded solely on attendance; no exams, essays, or projects were required.

I observed that many used the three-hour period to catch up on much-needed sleep while the teacher read sections of the textbook aloud in a monotone voice that lacked colour or enthusiasm. At the end of the lecture he told the students to read the same chapter before the following week's lecture.

My first thought was to turn down the college's offer. 'This is bullshit,' I thought, before accepting their offer on the practical basis that I was otherwise a rarely employed freelancer who already accepted bullshit assignments when they came my way from commercial clients. 'Why should teaching a bullshit course be any different?' I concluded. Besides, it'll help pay the rent next month.

I was provided a copy of the fulltime teacher's textbook within which his personal notes were indicated, in yellow highlighter, when and where he left off the previous week. I immediately placed the textbook in my desk drawer and never opened it again.

"Hello everyone. I'm Eddy, your substitute teacher for the next four weeks."

After introducing myself to the class at my first lecture, I instructed them to leave their textbooks at home for the duration and announced what I would be covering, and what I would be expecting from the students.

From the back row, a hand shot up and started waving. "Sir, Sir ... We're not supposed to be getting any assignments in this course."

'Great,' I thought. 'They haven't fallen asleep yet.' I pondered. 'Why do the smart-ass hecklers always shout from the back of the class and the quiet reserved ones sit up front?'

I answered the heckler. "That's OK. You don't have to do anything you don't want to do. However, this will be something you will all want to do." I clasped my hands together to emphasize my faked enthusiasm.

"What's it worth?" another student shouted from the back row.

"Your life," I answered with a stern face before it morphed into a silly grin.

"No. I mean how will we be graded?"

"Nothing. It's worth nothing. I'm not grading it. The true value of art shouldn't be based upon payment."

"Then why would we do it?"

"For self-satisfaction and personal exploration," I answered.

After a pause to monitor the silent response, I continued.

"During the next four weeks, you will have the wonderful opportunity to express yourself in whatever manner you choose. You can call it anything you want. You can even call it bullshit, but I will call it art. The only requirement is that you produce something that is important to you, something that means a lot to you."

The class remained silent until someone asked the inevitable question. "How will I know if it's art. I don't know nothin' about art."

"You will know when you get into it," I answered. "If you start to feel anything while you're making it that makes you laugh, cry, or fall in love, that's probably art."

"So, when my wife gets mad at me and starts screaming and throwing shit around, that's art?"

At least the heckler was listening to me. I opted to carry on without responding.

Instead of reading from the textbook like their previous teacher, an act that would guarantee they would hate the very word 'art' for the remainder of their lives, I showed slides of art objects made from car parts, sculptures from plumbing fittings, detailed arrangements of hunting and fishing paraphernalia. To demonstrate that art took many forms, I read selections from a Hemingway short story about fishing in the north country and a humorous excerpt from a Kurt Vonnegut sci-fi. I threw in some personal photographic images that were abstracted details from found objects: rust patterns on a dilapidated fishing boat, bird feces splattered on granite rocks that appeared ominously like a Jackson Pollock canvas, etc. There were also some slides showing the work of Indigenous painters who interpreted their visions and stories from their elders.

"So," one of the students proposed, "an old beater car or boat could be art. Is that what you're saying?"

"What makes it art is what it does to you, and for you, and how you interpret it. Was the old boat your grandfather's, for example? Is there a deep-seated memory or meaning to the old car? Is it the car you first made love to your wife in, or the car you went to Woodstock in? Or both, for that matter. That could be the source of art. All you have to do is find a unique way of seeing it, one that expresses your connection. It doesn't have to mean the same to a stranger as long as you feel something within yourself. With any luck the stranger will also feel something."

In the slide-watching darkness I heard murmurs and whispers shared between students.

"Shit, I've got one of them old Fords (Chevies, John Deeres, etc.) in the back forty that ain't been driven in twenty years." Another student offered, "My grandpa still has a 40-foot sailboat that he built by hand. It's sitting in the old barn now."

I responded to the anonymous murmurer. "Don't overlook the barn. It could have some deep-seated memories for you."

"Oh yeah. I could tell you stories from that barn that would curl your hair," the student offered.

One observant student suggested that I was asking them to get all emotional about something and that I wanted them to present it with tears in their eyes.

"Exactly," I agreed. "Or with a smile on your face. Maybe you want to make the world a better place with your art. Whatever. I do want you to let it all hang out. That's why you'll hand in a piece of your own creation and … wait for this … share what it means to you with the class."

"Fuck that," one hard-hearted soul proclaimed with his arms folded across his chest. "I ain't standing up there and cryin' my eyes out. No way … not in front of these guys."

"You don't have to. Give me something we can all laugh at instead."

* * *

Our second meeting was haphazardly planned, which was fortunate because I started the lecture with, "How are the projects going?" a question that encouraged an hour or two of discussion before I was able to start delivering my loosely prepared notes.

I was assaulted with a barrage of questions, concerns, and anxieties from the majority of the students.

"I can't think of anything to do," was a common theme.

"What if I start something and can't finish it by the deadline?"

"What if it's not art?"

"What if I don't like what I do … is it still art?"

To many of the questions, I had the answer. "Why does it matter whether it's art or not?" a response that I followed with, "A well-known Anishinaabe painter told me that, in his language, there is no word for art. The concept of art is included within their word for life. The same word also covers the concept of religion."

"There's a lot of different kinds of art," a student shouted bluntly. "That's what the other teacher told us." He starts counting on his fingers. "There's modern art, abstract art, romantic art, impressionistic art …"

"OK," I interrupted. "I get the message. The photographer, W. Eugene Smith once said, "Hardening of the Categories causes Art Disease."

A silence drops over the class like it's being sprayed with DDT. Their collective expression says, 'What the fuck is he talking about now?'

I continued, "Why does it even matter what kind of art it is, or whether it's art or not?" I added a 'food-for-thought' quote. "Art is Life, Life is Art."

To that, one of the challenging students offered with a grin, "If Life is Art, why don't we just show up for the deadline and present ourselves?"

I answered sarcastically, "If that makes you feel any better, then do it, but do it naked."

The entire class responded with laughter.

I broke into a broad grin as well, knowing that finally I have them on my side.

I continued with heightened confidence. "But, seriously guys … will you be happy just showing up with nothing but yourself? Sure, you'll still get the same grade as all the others, but will you get something out of it that's satisfying to *you*? … besides pissing me off because you're just being lazy, that is."

* * *

By the third week, the class dynamics were improving. There were projects in the works that made their questions and concerns more practical and functional.

A 40-something man named James approached me, preferring a one-on-one conversation. His brow was deeply furrowed and the lines on his face were hard-earned.

"Is it art if it comes from my memory?" James asked, with a caveat, "My memory ain't been so good lately."

"What do you want to do?" I asked.

James struggled with his words and they came out slowly. "I want to paint my grandfather's farm like I remember it when I was just a kid. The problem is that whenever I try to draw the buildings, I lose track of which were bigger and which were smaller. It's been a long time."

As my confidence heightened, my responses became less sarcastic and more contemplative. After silently considering James' concerns about scale, I offered, "How do you remember the buildings? Are some bigger than others in your memories? Regardless of what the scale was, your memories of the magnitude of each structure is the only issue of importance. Ask yourself why a simple shed may be more alive in your memory than a huge barn. What were your experiences in each of those buildings? Those are far more important than the realities of scale."

James questioned, "But I want to get it right."

"There is no right or wrong, James. How would you have painted them when you were a child? Would they all be correctly sized? Would the lines all be plumb and lined up with each other? Of course not.

Don't try to impose your current values as an adult on your memories. Our adult values are too restrictive and distorted by the life that got in the way since you were young. This assignment is not about how you see them now, as an adult. It'll be much better if you use your childhood memories. Allow the painting to be as free and whimsical as your memories."

* * *

Finally. Deadline Day. I arrived a half hour early and ordered a coffee. From my table in the cafeteria I could see down the corridor to the open door of our classroom. One by one, the students arrived, carrying their works of art under their arms. Some carried sketchbooks, others bore larger pieces like framed canvases. One rolled in a TV with a video player. Every student showed up and not one arrived empty-handed.

The first to present her work was Shinju, a Japanese student from the welding program. She arrived pushing a four-wheeled dolly that supported a sculpted open oyster shell constructed of sheet metal. It measured a metre in all three dimensions. In the centre of one of the oyster halves was a frosted glass globe. When the sculpture was placed as she insisted, light from the classroom window transmitted a glow through the frosted globe revealing a large pearl.

Shinju's story was fascinating. She recalled her family in Japan who were fishers, and how they struggled to provide her with the opportunity to study medicine abroad; she chose Canada. She explained that her name, Shinju, meant pearl in Japanese. Her parents named her that in hopes that she would give them good luck to find a valuable pearl in their nets someday. It was not to be, as Shinju felt she had disappointed her parents by failing out of medical school. She hoped to redeem herself by learning a trade before her student visa expired and she would be forced to return home to face her parents in Japan.

I applauded her with tears in my eyes; the class joined my enthusiasm.

"Now you can return home as an artist," I added.

* * *

James presented a watercolour interpretation of his grandfather's farm from an aerial perspective, in all its whimsical childhood glory. He included images of himself as a child, positioned at each of the outbuildings helping his grandfather with the chores applicable to the function of each building. He appeared on the back of an antique International tractor as he and his grandfather plowed the fields, and he's seen spreading food across the gravel parking lot for the chickens.

"I chose to show the farm from above as my grandfather might see it from heaven," James explained.

As his story unfolded, we learned of James' difficult life as the abandoned child of incarcerated parents. His grandfather took him in and raised him on the farm. His project was dedicated to his grandfather, the person who saved his life.

Unfortunately, life dealt James a second blow when his grandfather passed away unexpectedly; the farm was consumed by a greedy developer for taxes owing. A shopping mall now sits on the property where James helped his grandfather sow the seeds of a better life.

James ended up homeless on the streets of Toronto until the opportunity to attend college and learn a trade became a reality. All that remained of life on the farm for James were his memories, the whimsical childhood memories painted and preserved forever on a single piece of paper signed by the artist.

"You have to frame this, James," I told him. "It's a keeper. Hang it up somewhere where you can look at it every day."

Not a dry eye could be seen in the classroom.

* * *

Among the other works of art were a hand-scribed book of poetry for children, complete with watercolour illustrations on handmade paper; several paintings, large and small, from landscapes to abstracts; a videotaped re-enactment of a student and his girlfriend's first intimate encounter presented as a reality show. Only a short introduction of the video could be shown in class due to time and content restrictions.

The presentation class continued well after the three-hour limit. Nobody left the room for fear of missing someone's presentation. When all was done, I thanked everyone for making my experience one I would never forget.

"I assure you that I have learned as much as everyone else during the past four weeks. Thank you."

The heckler from the back row in the first class, who had, week by week, gradually moved up to the front row, stood to address the class and to conduct a "Hip, hip, hooray," before presenting me with a handwritten scroll bound with a red ribbon. It contained a signed petition from the entire class, proposing that the college should hire me as a fulltime replacement for the other teacher.

Lessons learned.

OF BODY AND SOUL

The 'Tempus Fugit' Jazz Bar is crammed with regulars: university students and professors, yuppies in suits, musicians, hookers, and a small gathering of doctors and lawyers. There are gyrators and finger-poppers, lovers, and thinkers; a typical Friday night.

Some women's husbands sit with other men's wives in dark corner booths, insulated by dense smoke that hangs at eye level like industrial smog. The heartbeat is hard bop. It slices through the haze, careens off dusty, photo-dotted walls, and penetrates the bodies and souls of everyone.

Jesse Townsend's tenor sax blazes through Giant Steps with confidence, as if hard-wired to Coltrane, its master. The deeper he delves inside, the further he edges outward, expanding the distance between him and the solid foundation of the rhythm section. The night burns on, driven by a unifying spirit.

At 68, Jesse owes dues to no one. He's worked with the best since the '50s when he played fourth tenor for Basie. He also worked two years on the road with Blakey and recorded with Mingus. He prefers, however, to front his own group around town. There are fewer hassles, less traveling, and he's free to pick his own tunes and sidemen.

The other horn player in the band is Jesse's long-time friend, trumpeter Freddy Harris. He and Jesse met on a session gig before Bird died and have worked together ever since. Freddy describes their association as, 'Siamese twins joined at the soul.'

The band's young rhythm section is handpicked from the latest crop of piss-and-vinegar kids from the music college. Jesse and Freddy represent a launching pad for their careers. Like a gauntlet placed between the classroom and the truths of life, the elders test the kids by shifting tempos, changing keys, and leading them into fresh harmonies, just to keep them listening. The musical puzzles are hard dues for the kids, but they keep the music alive for Jesse and Freddy.

Jesse steams into his final chorus of Giant Steps and the youngsters hang on, unwilling to break. He raises his right eyebrow. In a blazing flurry of arpeggios, Freddy slides through a turnaround and flies into his first chorus. Jesse smiles, and retreats to the back of the stand.

During intermission, Freddy mingles with some of the regulars at the bar. Jesse retires to his usual table, well hidden in a dark hallway that leads to the washrooms. Their personalities differ only in the ways they spend their social time. Jesse is thoughtful and pensive, preferring philosophical discussions with one or two people at a time. Freddy is more gregarious. His voice and boisterous laughter carry above the din of the club as he jives his way around, high-fiving from one regular to the other.

Waldo, the young pianist, is a classically trained musician who emigrated from Croatia to study composition at the college through an international scholarship. His intense desire to know everything about jazz draws him to Jesse's table at every opportunity, where he soaks up the master's words like a sponge.

Waldo has heard about a possible concert gig at the upcoming Summer Jazz Festival and proposes the idea to Jesse.

"I don't know, man," Jesse offers. "Concerts aren't what I'm into, you know what I mean? It's not the same as getting up here every night and working out. In the club you can be more adventurous with the music, stretch out, you know what I'm saying? There are no inhibitions about it being good or bad, or any of that shit."

Waldo suggests that it might be better to perform for people who really want to listen to the music, like at concerts, instead of playing to "a bunch of drunks and yahoos."

Jesse responds, "The thing isn't about who the audience is because it doesn't matter. We don't really do this thing for anybody else, we do it for us, man. In fact, it isn't even about 'doing,' it's about 'being,' you dig?" His voice speaks softly, and the phrases come out slowly, with long spaces between the words.

Waldo nods to acknowledge that he digs, but his quizzical expression reveals that he still has many questions. He wants to jump into the conversation during some of the pauses, but experience has taught him to exercise patience until Jesse completes his train of thought.

"What about doing a recording, Jesse? People would buy it for sure," Waldo interjects.

"You weren't listening, man. It isn't about them, it's about us, this thing we do. It's not about peddling merch, man. I knew a guy, some years back. He did a recording. The session sucked all the passion right out of him, and he never got it back. There was this engineer on the session that didn't know shit about the music. The whole thing ended up sounding like some cheap disco crap. After it was over, he never listened to the stuff again. What's the point in that, man? Just do the thing and do it for you. Everything you do is about here and now."

Waldo finally pleads, "What is this 'thing' you keep talking about, Jesse?" His arms gesture frantically and passionately in front of him. "What do you mean by the thing?"

"This thing ..." Jesse starts, hesitating to gather his thoughts together. "This thing comes from deep inside, and that's where it has to return to. You have to feed yourself, man, it's like protein. You need nourishment. You have to be a junkie for the music. That's all that counts." He pauses, and then adds, "It sounds selfish, I know man, but that's the way it has to be. It's the only way it works. You can't go around trying to figure out who's listening to what, or whether it's good or bad."

Jesse opens the next set with a free solo introduction to Body and Soul, a rite of passage for every tenor player since Coleman Hawkins. He weaves a unique palette of tonal colours through the changes, twisting and challenging, while still honouring the integrity of the ballad.

The mumbling conversation diminishes into silence, offering a shrine-like backdrop to this most sacred of jazz classics. All ears are focused on Jesse, hoping to share in the spirituality of his inner voice. Freddy stands back, still and quiet, in the shadows of the bandstand, his head bowed, and his eyes closed in meditation, receiving Jesse's messages in his own way.

Jesse surges into his second chorus when he suddenly stumbles into the kidney of the grand piano and leans his elbow against the edge. The sounds continue from his horn but the grimace on his face reveals his pain. He turns away from the crowd, pulls the horn from his lips and tumbles headlong into the bowels of the piano, issuing a final chord from hell. For a moment, the club comes to a standstill, as if frozen in time, like the photographs on the walls.

Freddy moves first. He grabs Jesse, firmly but gently laying him on the floor. "Jesse, for Christ's sake, man. What's wrong?" He turns to the crowd gathering around. "Give him space. He needs air."

Within minutes, the paramedics arrive and hustle Jesse off to the General Hospital. Freddy accompanies him in the ambulance, prodding at him constantly. "Get with it, man. Talk to me. Don't give up now."

At the hospital they hook Jesse up to oxygen and monitor his heart. The EKG metes out Jesse's life in a steady unrelenting tempo, '... bleep ... bleep ... bleep ...' The doctors pump and prod at his limp body. He's hanging on but he isn't coming to. The sound from the machine continues, steady, inflexible (more Bach than Bird). Freddy remains seated in a chair by his side.

Hypnotized by the repetitive pulsing, Freddy's mind plays with the tempo like he and Jesse played tricks with the young rhythm section in the band. He imagines new melodies over the rhythm and weaves fresh harmonies into them. Freddy delays the arrival of some bars and anticipates others while the tempo of the EKG remains as steady as a metronome. He syncopates punch notes against the time and imagines dissonant halftone clusters while he sits on a flatted ninth for bars over a bass lead walking beneath it. His internal band cooks from somewhere deep within.

Exhausted, Freddy dozes, with the melodies, rhythms, harmonies, and counterpoints burrowing into his subconscious half-sleep. Hours pass. The tunes drive deeper inside causing his teeth to grind involuntarily against the syncopated rhythms that become more outside and complex the longer they play within him. In his sleep he visualizes Jesse laying so calmly on the bed before him, his image burned onto the insides of his closed eyelids. The only sign of his existence is the mesmerizing '... bleep ... bleep ... bleep ... z-z-z-z-z-z-z-z-z-z-z-z-z, ...'

Doctors, respond quickly to the flatline, attempting to jump-start Jesse with a defibrillator. He bounces up hard each time before falling back into lifelessness.

The man who gave Freddy his first break into the business, the same man who gave him a reason to drag himself out of the gutter, is leaving and there's nothing he can do to change it. His own internal voice cries out in one last desperate appeal. "Jesse, for Christ's sake. Talk to me. Don't leave without talking to me, man. Give me a sign. Tell me you're still with me."

Before doctors can disconnect Jesse, Freddy hears the EKG blurting out a cacophony of sounds quite unlike the steady tempo of earlier. It's as if the machine is piping the sounds of Jesse's tenor directly into Freddy's soul. In a state of confusion, Freddy accepts the machine's erratic energy as a message from his lifeless friend.

The sounds from the machine organize themselves into a harmonic bliss that's shared only by the two old friends. Freddy recognizes the changes and pleads. "Take me with you, man! Wherever you're going, take me with you!"

The sounds draw Freddy slowly, but unrelentingly, upwards from his chair and he feels the mouthpiece of his own trumpet press against his lips. It's already warm. He picks up on the Coltrane changes to the bridge of Body and Soul, just where they left off at the club. Together again, they're creating beautiful, haunting sounds.

Freddy is struck with the reality that this will be their last chorus. There'll be nowhere to go after this, like driving down a one-way street past a 'no exit' sign. Just as the final cadence is about to close in on them, Freddy voluntarily removes the horn from his own lips to give Jesse the last word. Freddy listens intently, then grins. The grin widens into an internal laughter.

In its refusal to quit, Jesse's tenor carves through a series of turnarounds, modulating up a half tone and pulling the tune back to the top of the head.

"You did it, man. You pulled it off." Freddy replaces the trumpet to his lips and joins Jesse.

Throughout the night they wail together, modulating from one key to another, weaving in and out of meter, creating joyous fugal patterns of pure bliss. They play chorus after chorus, with Freddy grinning and groaning through it all. Repeatedly they arrive at what might become the final chorus, only to turn it around for yet another.

Time no longer has meaning beyond the steadiness of the implied rhythm. Whether minutes become hours, or hours become days, is of no significance. There are no nights, no mornings, no club owners, no cash registers, no pushers, no customers, and no requests. The eternal turnarounds ease them from one chorus to the next, each one probing into places previously unexplored. They wail looser, with more loftiness and confidence than they'd ever known in life.

* * *

The 'Tempus Fugit' Jazz Bar is crammed with regulars: university students and professors, yuppies in suits, musicians, hookers, and a small gathering of doctors and lawyers. There are gyrators and finger-poppers, lovers, and thinkers; a typical Friday night.

Some women's husbands sit with other men's wives in dark corner booths, insulated by dense smoke that hangs at eye level like industrial smog. The heartbeat is hard bop. It slices through the haze, careens off dusty, photo-dotted walls, and penetrates the bodies and souls of everyone.

Under Waldo's leadership, the new veterans in the rhythm section cook through their own recipe of Giant Steps, steering a couple of replacement horn players from the local music college through the heavy traffic. A young tenor player drives hard, trying to squeeze his entire 18-year life into one night. Waldo calls from behind the keyboard. "Ease up, man. There's no hurry. You're going to need that energy later … for Body and Soul."

SELF-INTOLERANCE

Nigel Pettycase lives the life accredited by neighbours who have just discovered that one of their own is a serial killer; one who has been burying the remains of his victims in his beautiful garden of chrysanthemums, after barbecuing and cannibalizing their vital organs. His life is, in a word, unassuming.

Like most of those hideous ghouls, Nigel regularly attends the church of his choice, even serving as an occasional Sunday school teacher and as an assistant Boy Scout leader with some distinction. Other aspects of his life are less visible as he maintains a bachelor's status of solitude, taking care of his dear mother in their shared two-bedroom, vinyl-sided bungalow on a suburban cul-de-sac that they have occupied since the death of his father, more than twenty years before.

His neighbours know him only as Mr. Pettycase, with conversation between them limited to an occasional, "Good morning. Nice day isn't it? Do you think it'll rain this afternoon?" Nigel always greets them with a moderate smile and a polite nod of acknowledgment. In colder weather he salutes his response by touching the thumb and forefinger of his right leather-gloved hand to the brim of his grey tweed fedora.

Unlike serial killers however, Nigel never exercises his frustrations by lifting a finger against anyone; violence is not his style. In fact, none of his neighbours ever remember him raising his voice, a voice so soft and quiet that oftentimes they fail to understand the words he utters, on the few occasions that he utters any at all.

Without fail, Nigel attends to his duties as a chartered accountant in the partitioned office of a large financial firm. The partitions assure that he has minimal contact with any of the company's clients.

Throughout his entire working life Nigel has risen at precisely six o'clock and, following his routine of shaving, showering, teeth flossing and brushing, has dressed in neatly pressed grey flannel trousers, a starched-collared, cuff-linked white shirt, and blue blazer. In later years he introduced an element of colour by sporting ties of mauves and maroons, gifts he received at Christmas and on birthdays from his mother, his only known living relative.

Unknown to many of his peers was his quiet, but active, political involvement in the 1960s. Out of a personal commitment to social issues, he appeared at peaceful demonstrations opposing injustices as varied as the war in Vietnam, horrific living conditions in Canadian First Nations, segregation in Alabama, and apartheid in South Africa. He carried no signs, but marched doggedly along, in the proud belief that his mere presence was a direct contribution toward ending intolerance forever. These are the memories from his past that he holds sacred within him and never talks about publicly.

Equally unknown are the many personal intolerances that he keeps so well-hidden inside that even he fails to recognize them. He maintains an uncomfortable aversion to certain mannerisms that people exhibit when they communicate: the ways they position their chins, place their hands, fold their arms, scratch their ears and noses, whether they cross their legs or spread them apart, how they point their forefinger for emphasis or rhythmically tap their fingernails on desks while impatiently waiting for a response. He often mutters to himself how much he hates it when people act this way or that way.

'God, how I hate it when waitresses smile at me when all they want is a good tip. It's all so phony. Why can't they just be themselves? And look at that man over there. He's folded his hand up under his chin as if he wants us to believe that he's deep in thought. And why, whenever the government changes something so they can steal more of our own money from us, do they always tell us that they're doing it for our convenience?'

On the day he retires, precisely on his sixty-fifth birthday, he receives the full benefits of his entire sick leave allowance, as he has not lost an hour in the twenty-seven years of his employment to even the slightest of ailments.

The management has to force him to stop working earlier than his usual six o'clock so they can acknowledge his many years of faithful service to the company. His co-workers, many who have rarely shared a conversation with him, gather around his partitioned desk. They present him with several gifts that he might find useful in his twilight years.

Of his private life, his co-workers only know that Nigel likes dabbling in a workshop located in the basement of his mother's house, where he manufactures a variety of wooden lawn ornaments, kinetic replicas of Freddy Flintstone, Disney characters, and geese, all with rotating legs and wings that respond to the wind.

They decide against presenting him with a gold watch in the belief that, because he is so obsessed with precision, he must already own several excellent timepieces. Instead, they present him with a shiny new Black and Decker 3/8-inch variable speed electric drill with his name, Nigel X. Pettycase, engraved on the handle. Throughout his entire career, nobody has mustered up enough courage to enquire about his middle name. Smaller gift-wrapped packages contain a complete set of drills and screw bits.

His secretary, who knows him as well as any, focuses a video camera on the proceedings so Nigel will have a permanent record of his important day. "Say a few words for posterity, Mr. Pettycase," she prods, encouraging the others to join in.

"Speech, speech," they encourage, clapping their hands together in the precise rhythmic unison expected from a group of accountants.

Unaccustomed to speaking in public, Nigel nervously stammers some appropriate words, or words that seem appropriate to him under the circumstances.

"Thank you … um … very much. It has been … um … wonderful knowing all of you … um … for these many years. I look forward to my … um … retirement and to the many leisure hours I will … um … spend in my workshop."

He manages to conceal his sadness at being forced to retire as he had always planned to spend the remainder of his useful years working. His ideal view of retirement would be to suddenly just fall gently forward at his desk when his time runs out.

In the weeks and months that follow, Nigel continues to rise at six o'clock without the aid of an alarm clock, just as he had done throughout his working life. Instead of walking to the office, he meanders endlessly through the streets of his neighbourhood. At noon each day he arrives at the park to share his brown bag lunch with the resident ducks. Weekends also remain the same. On Sundays, after church, he continues to prepare afternoon tea for he and his mother.

One rainy Saturday morning, several months later, Nigel decides to view the video his former secretary took during the retirement party. He thinks the first few minutes are quite funny and laughs aloud in his solitude; he has never seen himself on film before.

His laughter subsides however, when he first notices how he places his right leg over the left, an act that he never likes when other people do the same thing. He's also uneasy about how he places his left hand in front of his mouth when he's delivering the thank you speech. The more he sees of himself on the screen, the more he recognizes gestures and body language that he detests in others. He becomes agitated when he sees how his speech is interrupted by so many hesitations.

'Have I always done these things?' he asks himself. 'Have I always been such a klutz? How stupid I look.'

As the day progresses he replays the recording over many times, becoming angrier at himself with each viewing. Even after he stops the machine and retreats into his basement workshop to escape the agony of these new realizations, he can't erase them from his mind. He attempts to work the frustrations out by assembling a life-sized silhouette of a cowboy he plans to place next to the garage door. He affixes a Phillips screw bit into his new drill, hoping the sound of the drill will help him relax but the thoughts refuse to disappear. Instead, they become more intense. A stabbing pain invades his forehead.

* * *

From his horizontal position he senses the existence of a human figure wavering in and out of focus in front of him. The figure, silhouetted against a bright light, strokes his arm. Initially, he imagines the cowboy he'd been working on, but gradually changes his mind.

'It must be an angel,' he concludes. Minutes, maybe hours, pass before he hears the soft voice emanating from the haloed figure.

"Nigel … Nigel … Can you hear me?" the voice asks. "You are all right now. The worst is over."

With time, after much fading in and out, the image comes into focus.

"Where am I?" Nigel asks in a gravelly monotone voice.

"You're safe now. You've been through quite an ordeal, but you're safe now."

"Mother?" he asks. He sees her head nod affirmatively against the strong light. "Where am I?"

"You're in the hospital, Nigel. Everything will be all right." She continues to stroke his arm.

Nigel attempts to raise his head from the pillow, but it refuses to budge. "What am I doing here?" He raises his hand to feel the bandages on his head.

"Apparently you tried to commit …" Her voice breaks as tears flow down her cheeks, unable to finish the sentence. "Whatever possessed you to pick that drill up and …?" She pauses again. "Nigel, I can't believe you did this to yourself. I just don't understand it."

Some early details of the event start to focus for Nigel. He remembers watching the video, he recalls how he became so upset with his actions … and the stabbing pain. It will be a while before he can fully comprehend what he did with the electric drill but the seven holes in his scalp will never fully heal.

His mother regains her composure. “Of course, it’ll be some time before you can return to the house, Nigel, but they’ll take good care of you here in the meantime. Don’t worry about preparing afternoon tea, I can look after it myself.”

TALES FROM QUAGMIRE TOWNSHIP

A HISTORY OF QUAGMIRE TOWNSHIP

Quagmire Township occupies the entire land mass of an island in the upper great Lakes, but to call it an island is technically a misnomer. For portions of the year, it's a peninsula, attached to the mainland by a narrow stretch of land wide enough for a horse cart to travel, providing another horse cart isn't travelling in the opposite direction. Most of the year, however, it functions as an island with access by either a bridge or a sporadically operating ferry.

The perimeter of the township is comprised of rocky waterfront but for several thousand acres of sandy beach facing the west, where millennia of prevailing winds and rolling surf have pummeled the rocks into fine sand.

Inland, the terrain reveals a combination of rocky outcrops with thin topsoil and muddy swamps. Legends describe how grazing cattle have disappeared in the swamp.

There is evidence that, long before European settlers arrived, Indigenous families traversed and camped on the island enroute to more rewarding hunting prospects. For many years, however, it remained uninhabited until, following the American Revolution, the land was granted by the crown to Jackson L. Quigmare, for services rendered during the revolution; details of the services he rendered have never been revealed.

Jackson was the son of a wealthy, and loyal, contributor to the British cause. While Jackson personally had done nothing to deserve the land grant, his father lobbied the crown to give him something as far away from the rest of the family as possible. The remainder of his siblings were provided with large tracts of Nova Scotia waterfront.

Quigmare signed the land grant deed by misspelling his own name while drunk, as 'Quagmire.' Once arriving at his new holding, he recognized the uselessness of the terrain and concluded that the mis-spelled name was more appropriate than his own, so he legally changed his own name to Quagmire.

Most of his life was spent as an idle layabout, squandering his meagre portion of the family fortune on alcohol. As his fortunes dissipated, he sold off portions of the land, mainly waterfront parcels because, at the time, they offered the only public access to the township aside from the wagon trail causeway.

Quagmire's personal holdings diminished until he was left with a few hundred acres of waterfront and a large home more reminiscent of the colonial style from his native Connecticut. With some of the profit remaining, Quagmire developed the essentials of a town, with a hotel to accommodate occasional visitors and a tavern to satisfy their thirsts, and of course, his own.

Gradually the town expanded to include a blacksmith and a barber/dentist. In time, it attracted a variety of visitors, many drawn by the fishing opportunities and eventually was registered as Quagmire, the seat of Quagmire Township. J. L. Quagmire became its first mayor, remaining in the position for 20 years.

In time, a road network spread outward from the town of Quagmire to the waterfront dwellings, initially as a perimeter road and subsequently a series of crossroads for less patient travellers.

Today, Quagmire Township is an idyllic waterfront summer retreat catering to people from the large cities within a few hours' drive. The town of Quagmire boasts hotels, restaurants, a donut shop, boutiques, liquor and beer stores, a community hospital, a bowling alley/pool hall and a deep-water pier for sailors.

Tourists are attracted to numerous campgrounds and RV parks, and cottagers to their permanent million-dollar estates. The town of

Quagmire serves as their sole source of supplies where, for several months a year, the increase in traffic brings the town to a standstill.

The current population is a blend of old families and new residents, mainly retirees from the large cities who recognize the benefits of liquidizing their big-city homes and living comfortably off the profits in Quagmire.

Before Jackson Quagmire died in 1816, he commissioned a statue of himself waving a sword from atop a spirited steed and had it erected in the town square. A plaque identifies him as 'J. L. Quagmire, Founder and First Mayor of Quagmire Township.' The locals pass by the statue every day on their way to shopping and the post office without giving it a second thought. Seagulls, however, often seek respite on his head and shoulders leaving ample deposits of guano before departing.

Recently, in 2020, an elementary school student, while conducting research for a local history project, discovered that the father of the same J. L. Quagmire (Quigmare) was in fact, a spy for the revolutionaries against the crown's forces in the colonies. It was suggested that he was a close friend of George Washington, possibly even crossing the Delaware in Washington's own boat. It was also disclosed that he owned a flotilla of slave ships. J. L. himself, had no direct connection to his father's activities except to inherit a portion of the family fortune, which he drank away in the rustic solitude of Quagmire Township.

One Sunday afternoon, shortly after the research paper was posted on social media, students from the township and from further afield, gathered around the statue. With ropes, and the assistance of a Jeep Cherokee, the statue was toppled, with J. L.'s own sword severing his head as it struck the pavement.

Discussion followed about whether the council should rebrand the township and the town itself. Suggestions for a new name were invited and 125 responses received. One hundred and twenty recommended leaving the name as Quagmire, because it best described the township's unique terrain. It was also suggested that the humour associated with the current name proved beneficial to local commerce. The council voted and accepted the overwhelming advice.

The mayor, costumed for the occasion as a town crier, announced from the steps of Quagmire Town Hall, "Hear ye, hear ye. A vote has been taken, and we have concluded that the overwhelming response from our citizens cannot be ignored. The name of Quagmire will remain. After much discussion, the committee noted that, because the founder's name was not Quagmire, but 'Quigmare,' the name is not officially based upon the person in question, but upon the glorious landscape we all love and cherish. In coming to this decision, taxpayers will save thousands of hard-earned dollars in administrative costs by leaving the name as it stands. If there are any questions from the press, I will be happy to address them over a pint from my regular table at the Queen's."

BOTTLES

"Close the door, Chuckie," Jim orders while whisking loose remnants of hair from the mayor's shoulders. "It costs me a fortune to keep this air conditioning going. I can't afford to cool down the entire town. That should be the council's job, right Mayor?"

The Mayor responds. "Things are going to get a lot warmer in Quagmire Township yet, Jim, before it cools down, what with all them newcomers from the city causing a hike in house prices and demanding all new facilities like a wastewater plant and recycling blue boxes."

The mayor's face reddens as he continues, waving his arms about.

"Taxes are gonna jump through the roof, you just wait and see. It's got a lot of us old-timers all fired up, especially when we can't afford to buy a house anymore."

The mayor brushes a few wayward bits of hair from his plaid jacket and turns to the mirror to adjust what little remains on his head.

"Chuckie, I said close the door." Jim repeats.

"I'm sorry Jim, but I'm real p-p-pissed off," Chuckie stammers, his baseball-capped silhouette casting its shadow across the floor toward the chair where Jim is working.

Jim turns toward the front of his shop, his eyes passing through the window that, from his vantage point, reads:

JIM'S BARBER SHOP

NO STYLES – JUST HAIRCUTS

THREE BARBERS – NO WAITING

Stylists at a couple of new shops had forced Jim to lay off the other two barbers before Christmas. All that remains are the three chairs, and Jim, but there's still no waiting.

"Damn it, Chuckie. Just come in and close the door."

Chuckie slams the door shut and shuffles his feet across the hair-laden linoleum and sits down next to the table of men's magazines. He picks up a year-old copy of Field and Stream, flips through the pages, then tosses it back onto the table. "Yup, I'm real p-p-pissed off, Jim."

Jim nods to the next customer. It's Ben Flaherty from the real estate office. Ben carefully removes his brindle-shit beige jacket, his brass name tag scattering a ray of reflected light around the shop before coming to rest on the coat rack. He squeezes his substantial buttocks into the chrome and cracked faux leather chair, moving them from side to side before settling into the most comfortable position. Jim flicks the sheet up until it snaps in the air. It falls down slowly, like a parachute, over Ben's torso. Jim pins the corners together behind Ben's neck.

"So, Chuckie. What's pissing you off?" the realtor asks.

Chuckie wipes the snot from his nose along his sleeve. "It's Walter, that goddamned new guy that hangs around up at the donut shop. You know that guy, eh Jim?"

Ben probes further. "There's lots of new folks in town, Chuckie. Which one is Walter?"

"That big guy with the baggy pants. Remember that guy, Jim? He was in here a few weeks back for a haircut, said he came from the city. Asked you for a job cleaning up and stuff. You was real good to me Jim, telling him you already had all the help you needed. Anyway, he's working at the donut shop now, cleaning up and stuff."

"So why does that piss you off Chuckie?" Jim asks. "You aren't working there too, are you?"

"No Jim. That don't bother me at all, but he's picking up bottles. I saw him last night down near the park. That's where I find most of my own bottles, Jim. He can't just come in here like that and take away all my business. Can he Jim?"

Ben Flaherty puts in his two cents worth. "That's exactly what happened when that fancy donut shop arrived here a couple of years ago. Two local businesses went belly-up within a month."

"Aw. Come on, Ben," Jim responds. "Those two places were just holes-in-the-ground. They didn't have nothing on that new shop. Half the time they didn't have any donuts, or they'd run out of coffee. Besides, their washrooms were filthy and clogged up half the time."

Ben remains uncharacteristically quiet.

Jim turns toward Chuckie, who's now engrossed in the centrefold of Hustler magazine.

"Speaking of coffee, Chuckie. How'd you like to run up and get us all a coffee? Just take a few Toonies from the till."

Ben interrupts. "Leave me out. I refuse to drink any of that swill from the new donut shop. Just on principle."

"Come on Ben," Jim shoots back. "What are you complaining about? At least you got your fat commission when you sold them the property, didn't you?"

Chuckie pushes NO SALE on the cash register and stares into the drawer. He pulls out a fiver and holds it up for Jim to see. "Is this right, Jim? Did I do okay?"

Jim nods. "You done good, Chuckie. Now go get the coffee. Just get two large black ones and grab a bunch of sugars and creamers. We'll fix them up here. Oh, here's another fiver, pick up a few of those walnut crunchy donuts too. Wait, on second thought, just get two. Ben doesn't need any more calories."

Along the three-block route to the Donut Emporium, Chuckie is constantly on the lookout for bottles: beer bottles, wine bottles, and any other kind of bottle that he can cash in. He focuses his eyes on the curbsides, probes into alleyways, peers under verandahs and sifts through bushes and shrubbery. His eyesight is so keen that he can identify a refundable bottle at forty paces without squinting, even at night. His gait is angular and irregular in tempo, meandering from one edge of the sidewalk to the other.

His keen eyesight spots Walter sweeping up the parking lot of the donut shop with a broom and dustpan. As he passes, Chuckie mumbles, just loud enough for Walter to hear. "You b-b-bastard."

Walter stops sweeping and places his hands on his wide rounded hips, responding to Chuckie in a slow, deep voice, "What's your problem?"

"There's not enough bottles in this town for both of us. You better screw off back to the city," Chuckie orders, shaking his forefinger. "It's because of you that folks can't afford a house anymore."

Walter's large frame, exaggerated by a combination of ill-fitting clothes, becomes more menacing when he raises the broom above his head, threatening to swing it against the side of Chuckie's head. In his deep slow voice he warns, "This is my territory." He hesitates to ponder his next sentence. "You better stay away from here, that's all I can say to you."

Chuckie cowers, stammers some mumblings back at Walter, and slips into the donut shop.

To avoid another confrontation with Walter on his return trip, Chuckie leaves by the opposite door next to the drive-thru window.

Between the dumpster and the fence around the parking lot, Chuckie discovers a stash of beer bottles. Armed with the full knowledge that they must have been hidden there by Walter and convinced within himself that he is the sole owner of any bottles found within the town limits, he carefully places them in the green army satchel that he always carries across his shoulder for such unexpected treasures and disappears down a back street.

"He was going to smash my head in, Jim," Chuckie complains when he arrives with the coffees and donuts. He shakes with a combination of excitement and fear while exaggerating his confrontation, as if an electrical current is passing through his body.

"You know, Jim, that Walter's a pretty big guy. But I think I can outsmart him, Jim. What do you think?" Chuckie emphasizes 'outsmart' by directing his forefinger toward his temple.

"You can do anything you want to if you put your mind to it," Jim acknowledges.

Ben Flaherty raises his torso from the chair. "Chuckie, anytime you need help from me, you just ask for it. Ain't no city boy gonna push you, or anybody else, around, you understand?"

Chuckie nods to Ben that he understands and returns to his Hustler magazine.

Jim whisks the loose hair from Ben's cape before snapping it away. He collects his five dollars and warns, "Don't you go starting anything, Ben. Chuckie can solve his own problems. Isn't that right Chuckie?"

Chuckie nods, this time to Jim, his eyes still fixed on the centrefold.

Back at the donut shop, Walter steps in to collect his free coffee and donut after sweeping up the parking lot. He's furious. "Who took all my bottles, the ones I hid out behind the dumpster?" he barks to the donut server behind the counter.

"It wasn't me, Walter," she replies. "I've been stuck in here all day."

Walter stomps his oversized boots in frustration. His face turns scarlet, fuming over his loss. He accepts his earnings and occupies an empty seat next to Bernie, an ex-pat New-Yorker and self-proclaimed artist who arrived in Quagmire a decade ago. He survives on the alimony he receives from Trish, his ex-wife, a corporate lawyer who, in university, fell in love with his artiness and pot-smoking. Since arriving in Quagmire, Bernie has managed to wean himself away from pot by adopting a prolific caffeine habit, most of it consumed during his multiple daily visits to the donut shop.

"How're you'se doing Bernie?" Walter starts.

Folding the top half of the Globe and Mail's arts section toward him, Bernie peers at Walter over his half-frame reading glasses. "What's the problem, Walter?" he inquires. "You look mad as hell."

"Somebody stole all my bottles. I need them so I can put more money in my bank account. I want to buy a trailer for my mountain bike …" Walter pauses to catch his breath. His face reddens and his usual monotone drawl picks up the pace, causing his words to run together like a speeding train coming to an abrupt stop.

He chatters on, "… so I can carry more bottles at a time. I only need 27 more dollars. Then I'll have enough. It's a great trailer too. I saw it at Canadian Tire. I'm gonna get a red one to match my bike. What do you think, Bernie?"

"I think you should find the bastard who stole your bottles, then beat the shit out of him. That's what I think." The edges of Bernie's lips rise into a smile as he delivers the solution.

The red in Walter's face intensifies. "Thanks Bernie, I'll do that. But who would steal my bottles? There's just me and Chuckie that collects them." Suddenly, Walter's eyes come alive.

"Wait a minute!" He slams his fist down onto the table as he recounts his altercation with Chuckie earlier in the parking lot. "That's it. It's Chuckie. He said I stole his bottles, and I never did, Bernie. Really, I found them bottles all by myself." He stuffs the remnants of his chocolate banana cream into his mouth, washes it down with coffee, and bolts out into the searing afternoon sun.

Bernie watches through the window as Walter's baggy pant legs propel his cumbersome frame down Main Street toward his destination. Bernie shakes his head and laughs aloud. "I was just kidding," he chuckles before returning his attention to the arts section of the paper.

* * *

It's the July long weekend. Familiar locals congregate around the benches in front of the Quagmire post office. Their normally fixed positions are momentarily altered to avoid being struck by a low-crotched skate boarder flinging himself and his board upward from the sidewalk in a vain attempt to balance atop the handrail. The boarder picks up his lacerated remains from the steps, remounts, and continues clattering down the street toward his next challenge.

Regulars continue to enter the Queen's Hotel for their afternoon refreshments. One suit-clad regular who has already exceeded his limit, exits, stops to adjust his tie and straighten his hair by carefully admiring his own reflected image in the window, turns and stumbles down the concrete steps onto the sidewalk. He slowly lifts himself, whisks the dirt from his suit with his hand, and proceeds to waver in the opposite direction from the skate boarder.

Like great endless serpents, unbroken lines of cars, motor homes, pickups and boat trailers wend toward their destinations in both directions down the heat-heaved pavement.

Walter wonders where all the people from the vehicles go. 'There ain't no parking spots available, and they ain't going into the stores.'

This temporary diversion almost interrupts Walter's real purpose for hurrying, until he arrives at the barbershop. Chuckie and Jim are staring out the window of the empty shop with coffees in their hands. When Chuckie notices Walter's face on the other side, he runs to hide behind the barber chair.

Walter becomes furious at the sight of Chuckie and begins shouting at him through the window from the sidewalk. His frustration causes his body to tremor and his face glows red with fury as he presses it against the glass.

Chuckie responds, "I'm the b-b-bottle king of this town. Go back to where you came from."

Walter starts hopping from one foot to the other. He raises his finger in a rude threatening gesture and sticks out his tongue.

In a defensive move, Chuckie grabs one of the contested bottles from his satchel and hurls it toward his adversary, smashing Jim's front window.

Fortunately, Walter sees it coming and pulls his face back from the glass before the bottle whistles past him to careen off the fender of a passing Audi before settling, undamaged, at curbside.

The Audi screeches to a halt and is immediately rear-ended by a Jeep Renegade laden with campers on their way to a boozing weekend at the campground. Three cases of beer refuse to stop as abruptly as the Jeep and their contents empty across the roadway. The Audi's irate pilot ejects himself from his vehicle, slams the door, and begins cursing to all within earshot. The obscenities devolve into uncontrollable sobbing once he assesses the damage to his vehicle.

The blood that flows freely from several lacerations on Walter's cheek doesn't inhibit his desire to help the innocent victims. He runs to assist the Jeep riders, who are already more than well lubricated, retrieve their wayward bottles. Chuckie, believing that Walter is gathering them for his own selfish reasons, makes a hasty decision to claim as many as possible for himself.

Jim stares, in disbelief, at the escalating conflict through his shattered barbershop window.

Ben, who is just entering the Queen's for his afternoon pint when the fracas erupts, yells into the crowded bar, "Hey everybody. They're ganging up on Chuckie. He's gonna need our help." The regulars, in varying degrees of inebriation, pour out into the street and begin tossing bottles about, with little regard to their intended targets. Glass is strewn everywhere.

Walter goes about his business of placing the few intact bottles he can retrieve into the rear of the Jeep. The Audi driver regains his anger and begins throwing bottles at the Jeep driver and at Chuckie, the source of his problems.

Just as the supply of available weapons becomes scarce, Ben drags cases of empties from the Queen's to re-arm the troops. From the north end of town, a corps of clients from the donut shop marches into the foray to protect their friend, Walter, who appears to be severely outnumbered. Quagmire's main street becomes a battleground, the two sides now evenly distributed between the locals, who support Chuckie, and the newcomers, who back Walter up.

Tourists, realizing they'll be stranded in traffic for some time, and fearing for their own safety, seek shelter in the myriad of gift shops, boutiques, health food stores and pharmacies. Once safely contained inside the stores, their insatiable desire to spend vacation money overtakes them. Items that have been sitting on shelves for years are purchased as gifts for mothers, fathers, aunts and uncles.

"They'll never believe this back in the city unless I get some pictures," one Tilley-clad Robert Capa wannabee with a point-and-shoot camera utters. He plunges out into the combat zone, zigging left, then zagging right, before strategically positioning himself behind a blue recycling box.

Police Sergeant Bellamy first hears about the melee while parked at the donut shop drive-thru. When he realizes Walter is involved, he decides against calling the incident in to the station until he has a chance to assess the situation. "Besides," he reasons, "the other cruisers are all occupied down at the campground for the long weekend."

Unable to maneuver his cruiser out of the drive-thru into the traffic jam, he borrows Walter's mountain bike from the back of the donut shop. Some locals chuckle at the short-panted sergeant attempting to manipulate Walter's red bicycle through crowds of amateur guerrilla fighters while ducking the foaming missiles.

Walter, upon seeing Sergeant Bellamy, and afraid that he's done something wrong, slinks into the alley and escapes northward to the donut shop without notice.

Chuckie limps off at great speed in a southerly direction to escape the Audi driver, who has completely lost control. Hurling stray bottles ahead of him at Chuckie, he finally gives up the chase three blocks later after losing his footing on some spilled lager and slicing his knee open against the glass while rolling downhill toward the harbour. Chuckie manages to avoid capture by slipping into the laundromat, concealing himself inside Maytag Dryer #6, where he remains until the early hours of the morning.

Darkness has taken over when the police from the campground finally arrive; the main drag of Quagmire is as quiet as a morgue. Yellow tape is stretched across both ends of Quagmire so that even the tourists can't retrieve their vehicles until the following day, which proves to be profitable for the bed-and-breakfast operators.

From his seat at the donut shop, Walter witnesses the occasional straggler wending his way home in the darkness. As the hours pass, the numbers become fewer. Convinced that everything is safe, Walter ventures out toward the centre of town. The streets are littered with debris, bits of broken bottles, half-torn labels of all brands, and bottlenecks with and without caps. The sponge soles of Walter's large shoes stick to the pavement with every step he takes. He can't believe the damage.

'Are people crazy?' he questions, to himself, without fully acknowledging the depth of his own role in the previous day's events.

Occasionally he stoops to pick up unbroken bottles, which he adds to his cache, strategically hiding them in flowerbeds and behind bushes and shrubs until he can retrieve them later.

Outside of Jim's Barber Shop, Chuckie stoops over some unbroken bottles, which he relocates into the shop, placing them behind the third chair, which isn't used anymore. He's certain they'll be safe there, at least until he can cash them in.

He sees Walter rummaging through the debris and approaches him from the north. "They're going to be real p-p-pissed off at us in the morning," Chuckie shouts to him from a safe distance. His voice echoes through the stillness.

Walter looks toward the voice and sees Chuckie stowing the bottles away. "What are we gonna do? The whole street's a mess."

"I don't know but Jim don't have no insurance for the window, so whatever I get from these bottles I'm gonna give to Jim for his window."

Walter starts to pick up some of the bottles in front of the barbershop. Chuckie raises his right hand, threatening to throw a bottle at him, but Walter catches him by surprise. "Don't worry Chuckie. We're in this together. We gotta help Jim out. Hurry with these so we can get the glass off the streets before the town wakes up."

Chuckie retrieves a couple of brooms from the closet in Jim's shop and they begin pushing broken glass from the centre of Main Street into piles next to the curbs.

"What do you think all these bottles would be worth if they weren't all smashed?" Walter asks.

Chuckie replies, "I don't wanna think about it, 'cause it would p-p-piss me off."

By daybreak, after they had moved all the glass into piles against the curbs, they find themselves in front of the donut shop. Walter thinks for a moment, and then turns to Chuckie. "I got an idea," he says, pointing to the side of his head. "Why don't we go inside? I'll buy you a coffee."

They order a couple of coffees and a dozen donuts. "Put it on my tab," Walter instructs.

They join Bernie, the artist, sitting in his usual seat. Walter asks, "What're you still doing here Bernie?"

"I couldn't sleep, so I decided I might as well start the day early. What are you guys doing here?"

"Me and Chuckie, we're startin' a business."

Over their caffeine and sugar-powered breakfast, and with Bernie's advice, they agree to form their own company and to sign a contract with the town to keep the streets clear of bottles. Walter will control all areas north of the post office, and Chuckie will take care of the southern zone. The money from all of the bottles collected by both of them will go into a joint bank account.

With the first light of dawn, the tourists start gathering to retrieve their vehicles. The Jeep driver spent the night in the same bed-and-breakfast as the Audi pilot. They met over breakfast, where they discovered their mutual fascination with chess and agreed to meet back in Toronto for a match.

Hidden by the shadows in the alleyway, Sergeant Bellamy has been covertly watching Walter and Chuckie clean up the streets. He chooses not to charge them for any of the damage. In fact, the only real damage inflicted by either one of them was when Chuckie hurled the beer bottle at Walter, breaking Jim's window, which the two bottle collectors promise to reimburse him for.

The sergeant charges the Jeep driver with following too close. He ignores the impaired driving charge when he sees him shaking hands with the owner of the Audi.

Ben Flaherty, who's partially responsible for inflaming the crowd, volunteers one of his vacant storage units as the warehouse for the new bottle business.

The Quagmire Township Better Business Association supplies a truck to take away the debris. They also donate a thousand dollars to Walter and Chuckie's new business in appreciation for the extra tourist business created during the battle. The mayor suggests that the battle be recreated as a tourist attraction each year on its anniversary. Council passes the suggestion on the basis that it will encourage recycling. They also approve the contract offer from Walter and Chuckie.

CRUISIN'

Thurston Penner is shocked awake by a shotgun blast outside his apartment window.

"Jesus Christ," he shouts, struggling with a pair of pants before checking it out.

Below, Jeremy sits on the horn of his 1968 Dodge Dart Fastback Sport Deluxe. He yells through the driver's window. "C'mon Thurston, old buddy. Get your sorry ass movin'. We don't have all night. We're goin' cruisin'." He lays on the horn again.

"Will you shut the fuck up. I was trying to sleep. And get that muffler fixed? I thought somebody was shootin' at me, man."

They load the vehicle with a case of 'two-four' and some extra cans of IPA and leave for a night of cruising the quiet back roads around Quagmire Township.

Thurston shouts. "Wait, stop the car, Jeremy. I just remembered. I've got a bottle in the apartment that Tubby Little gave me the other day. I'll get it. He traded it for my Ford carburetor. You remember that old Ford I used to have, right? I finally got rid of the last part. I told him it's all seized up, but he didn't care. Gave me a bottle of bourbon for it."

"I think you got shafted Thurston. Tubby can fix anything; you should know that. Don't matter what it is, he can fix it. Get that bottle anyway. We can use it. I'll wait for 'ya."

They head out Mountain Road, which leads to a slight rise in the topography. Locals call it a mountain because it's the closest thing there is to one in the township. Once past the cemetery they veer right on freshly gravelled Perimeter Sideroad, spewing a cloud of dust and rocks behind them. Jeremy pulls the headlight switch. Only the left bulb lights, pointing upward at forty-five degrees into the darkening night sky as if searching for enemy planes. The right headlight had been lost completely when the Dodge careened off a tree during an earlier cruise, ripping the entire fender from the body. Jeremy managed to reassemble the parts using baling wire and duct tape.

"It's my early warning system," Jeremy says, "just in case the screws come in by helicopter."

Thurston laughs. They pull out the first couple of beers, sucking back the entire contents within minutes.

"Pass me another one of those," Jeremy orders to his friend. They toss the empties out into the dust. "I always practice sorting and recycling; the cans get tossed out the driver's window and the bottles go out the passenger's."

"Chuckie does the recycling," Thurston replies with a grin as he raises the bottle to his lips. "You just look after the sorting."

"You know, Thurston. This is the best damned car I ever owned," Jeremy brags. "They don't come any better than this. Since I got it I've put on more than a hundred thou and it had more than that when I bought it from the wrecker for two hundred bucks — and them's miles, not klicks. Man, did I get a deal or what?"

Thurston points out some of the car's disabilities. "You should really get Tubby to look after that light," he jokes. "Like you said, Tubby can fix anything. And get him to do somethin' about that muffler, and this seatbelt; it doesn't even work. What if the cops stop us?"

"They don't bother coming down these roads 'cause nothin' ever happens down here, and they don't want to get their shiny cruisers dirty. Besides, I don't use seat belts. Ain't nobody gonna tell me what I can or can't do. It's a stupid fucking law, just like the biker's helmet law. You'd think we were living in a communist country with all these laws they make. Seat belts are for sissies anyway. We never needed 'em all those years before. Why in hell do we need 'em now?"

Thurston unscrews the cap on the bourbon and draws a long haul from the bottle. "Man, that's sweet. Here Jeremy, pull on this." He passes the bottle to the driver who repeats the motion and wipes his lips with his shirtsleeve.

Jeremy changes the subject. "Did you see that thing in the magazine at the supermarket about Cicely Black? Man, she's a hot piece of work. You remember her? She was the star in that vampire flick. It said in the paper that she's got the hots for a halfback with the Chicago Bears. They had a picture of her in a bikini on the front page, falling all over that guy. Man, is he a big sucker or what?"

Thurston offers, "A guy in town told me she bought a waterfront estate here on the Island, just over by Maple Point. He said she comes here every summer to get away from it all."

"There's all kinds of famous people here, man. Everybody knows that." Jeremy says. "Like that big estate on North Lake where they have the parties all the time. I heard that used to belong to Elizabeth Taylor. I don't know for sure but that's what they say."

"And *they're* usually right, eh Jeremy? We should cruise over past Maple Point and look for Cicely Black's place. I bet she's here for the long weekend."

The seed is planted. They gulp back a hearty swig each of the bourbon and snap caps from a couple of IPAs to wash it down.

"She's got a sweet set of hooters," Jeremy says between drinks. "You shoulda seen that picture in the paper. Whooey! They're out to here." He removes both hands from the steering wheel and positions them well out from his chest. The Dodge swerves in the loose gravel until he regains control.

Thurston contests their authenticity. "Aw, they're probably fake. You know, they do all kinds of things to make 'em bigger these days. Remember those chicks in 'Babe Watch?' You don't really think they're all real, do you? Sometimes they even fix up the pictures so they look bigger."

"No. They're really that big." Jeremy repeats his gesture with his hands. "It wasn't only the picture in the paper, but they were also huge in the movie too. Don't you remember?"

They continue fantasizing while the Dodge heads toward the waterfront. The Maple Point Road leads off the usual cruising route into a dead-end cul-de-sac, winding along the water's edge. Entry to the exclusive area is through two stone pillars with permanently opened gates attached, and a sign that announces the Maple Point Estates and warns trespassers that the premises are protected by law and video cameras. Jeremy grinds the Dodge Dart to a stop.

"C'mon Thurston. Let's get our picture taken by the security camera."

The paved road is separated from the water on the right side by a manicured grassy strip lined with mature maple trees that protect the roadway from the wind that blows in from the lake. On the left side, large well-treed lots disguise the over-priced summer homes from public view.

"Jesus, I wonder which one of these castles is hers," Thurston asks, in awe at the magnitude of the houses. "I ain't been down here in years. These places must be worth a couple million apiece. There ain't no mailboxes either. How're we gonna know which one is hers?"

Some houses sit in dark anonymity; others sport an assortment of Jaguars and Mercedes in their driveways. One mansion, with tall circular towers is alive with music booming into the otherwise still night. Expensive vehicles crowd out from the driveway onto the shoulders of the road.

Jeremy pulls his rusty Dodge Dart onto the grass. "Come on. There's a party going on. Let's check it out."

"Are you crazy, man? Thurston resists. "They'll never let us near the place, especially with this piece of junk. Look at these cars. Christ man, there's a Porsche and ... hey, check this out Jeremy. This is a Maserati. Y'ever seen one of them before?"

Jeremy's door squawks like a Canada goose when it opens. He starts walking up the cobblestone driveway. "Come on, Thurston.

Nobody will even care that we're here. There must be a hundred people in there."

Thurston reluctantly follows behind Jeremy. They sneak around to the back where crowds of people schmooze in small groups at the edge of the pool. The music is loud and pulsating. A massive stone barbecue with shimmering coals glows in a corner next to the house. A solid hulk of a man sporting an apron imprinted with 'The Hell With Housework' serves humongous steaks to the guests. Hair grows up his back and continues over his neck, stopping where he shaves his head.

Thurston cups his hand over his mouth and whispers to Jeremy, "Look at that big fucker over there by the barbecue pit. How'd you like to face him in a fight?"

Jeremy coughs, choking on his own laughter. "That's him. That's the guy from the Chicago Bears. Remember the picture I told you about? This has to be Cicely Black's place. Man, oh man, did we luck out or what?"

"Let's split up and see if we can find her. She's gotta be here somewhere."

Jeremy agrees. "Sometimes you're smarter than you look. Even if we don't find her, there's lots of other good stuff to look at. Have you ever seen so many great lookers in your life? Check out that blond playing horseshoes. Hot damn!"

The two separate and Thurston heads for the bar. He pours a quantity of Merlot into a beer stein and tries to hide himself amid a group of actors complaining about residuals, bored because he doesn't know the meaning of the word. He wanders to the edge of the pool to stare at the skin.

Jeremy leaves the horseshoe pitch after the blond of his dreams leaves in the arms of her companion. Nobody takes any notice of the local township boys until Jeremy starts talking up a shapely, but leathery-skinned, woman in a flowered bikini. "Have you seen Cicely around?" Jeremy asks.

"Can I help you?" she enquires, looking him up and down. "I'm

Cicely. What can I do for you?" Thinking that Jeremy might be one of the men hired to clean up after the party, she requests that he return later.

Jeremy's mouth hangs open in shock, first because he's actually talking to the famous actress, second, because she doesn't look anything like she did in the pictures, and third, because she just asked him to come back later. He tries to answer her, but no words materialize. Suddenly he's face-to-chest with the 'Hell With Housework' footballer.

"What the hell is going on? Who the Christ are you?"

Cicely interjects, "It's okay hon, the man's just leaving. He's one of the cleanup crew."

The guy grabs Jeremy by the arm. "No asshole is going to mess with *my* woman. Get the hell out of here." He tightens his grip on Jeremy's arm to escort him to the parking lot, shaking him until he rattles. Jeremy's feet barely scratch the ground.

In the shadow of a large maple tree, the Chicago Bear sees the silhouetted figure of Thurston relieving himself with a steady steaming stream against the front wheel of a Porsche Targa.

"What the hell?" the big guy bellows in a deep resonating voice. Thurston is caught in midstream and can't stop the flow. The man picks him up with his free arm, forcing Thurston to leak across the Porsche's mirror, over his baggy pants, and onto the man's apron. Furious, the footballer throws the two into the cobblestones and gives them each a solid kick with his size eighteen Nikes.

Jeremy and Thurston crawl the rest of the way to the Dodge to make their getaway. The doors squawk as they enter. From the open window Jeremy flicks the bird and shouts, "I'll tell the world that Cicely's boobs are fakes."

With a cloud of black exhaust, they peel the wreck down the driveway and into the darkness, the right fender flapping. They remain silent until they hit the gravel road.

Jeremy's the first to speak. "Man, was that Cicely broad ugly; nothing like her pictures. You can't trust anything anymore."

Thurston just groans, and then belches from the stein of Merlot that didn't blend well with the bourbon and the IPAs.

Jeremy continues. "I mean, she wasn't really that ugly. Her body was in pretty good shape, but her skin was wrinkled like a raisin. She must lie under sun lamps all day. Her hooters weren't as big as they were in the pictures either."

Thurston responds again with a weaker groan. "I don't feel so good Jeremy. Maybe we should head back to town. I think that big guy musta busted some of my ribs."

Jeremy objects, "No way are we going home yet; we're just getting started. What a night, eh? You'll be all right after a while. Here, have another beer. It's good for fixing up a hangover."

Not sure why he should believe his buddy, Thurston obeys by snapping a cap and sucking at the contents.

Jeremy points the Dodge down Ridge Road. "How's our booze holding up?" he asks his passenger. "Do you think we should stop in at the bootlegger's?" His driving is becoming erratic. He rubs at his eyes to sharpen their focus. As the car starts a downslide over the peak of a hill, he sees a figure along the side of the road. "Look at that Thurston," he points. "Who's that down there?"

Thurston groans in pain and rubs his eyes. He strains to see a lean figure limping along the roadside shining a flashlight into the ditch. "That looks like Chuckie. What the hell is he doing way out here at this time of the night?"

Jeremy slows the car down to get a clearer look. "It's Chuckie alright. He's picking up his bottles, man. Let's have some fun."

Through the open windows Jeremy yells, "Hey Ch-Ch-Chuckie! How's it g-g-going?" The car slows to a crawl.

Chuckie looks up from his duties to see who's calling his name. He waves to acknowledge them.

Thurston laughs at him. G-g-getting lots of b-b-bottles Chuckie?"

Chuckie shakes his flashlight at them. "G-g-go away. I'm busy earning a living. Why don't you g-g-go and get a job."

"Oh. Is Ch-Ch-Chuckie upset?" Thurston imitates, throwing an empty bottle toward him. "P-p-pick that one up, Chuckie. It's worth a fortune."

Jeremy sucks the last drop from his bottle and tosses it into the ditch. "There's another one Ch-Ch-Chuckie."

"G-g-go away. Leave me alone," Chuckie pleads.

The two yahoos laugh at him again. Jeremy puts his foot to the mat, spreading a gravel shower toward Chuckie, who throws himself into the ditch for protection. Once the Dodge is safely down the road, Chuckie searches for the two empty bottles to add to his collection.

Jeremy's control over the car is unsteady but he manages to keep it on the road. Suddenly, ahead of them, a large 14-point buck meanders into their path.

Thurston shouts, "Christ man, look at that. It's Bar-B-Q time. What you see when you don't have a gun, eh?"

Jeremy reacts much quicker than his inebriated state would normally allow. "Get ready for some venison, buddy, and hang on."

The buck ventures out further into the road and stops, staring into the mal-aligned headlight. Jeremy aims the Dodge as carefully as his current state will permit. "I got him in my sights. I'll try to get him with the bad fender, so I don't wreck my car."

All Thurston can do is to grab the handle of the door and bend down into the seat. "Are you out of your mind? That bad fender's on my side."

The buck remains frozen. His eyes shine like diamonds in the wayward beam of light. The Dodge lunges forward. Jeremy can already taste the venison; his mouth waters in anticipation. Contact is only a millisecond away when the buck lowers his rear flank and springs out of the path, disappearing rapidly into the bush. Jeremy makes one quick attempt to follow the buck, but the Dodge fails to respond. The front wheels lock themselves into a spin and the car veers sideways toward the edge of the road, spinning a 360 before settling its rear end in the ditch.

Minutes pass before the two regain their already limited sense of reality. Thurston, still bending over in his seat, hears the driver's door squawk open. He looks up. Jeremy is wandering in a random pattern in the middle of the road. Once he gathers his thoughts together he returns to the driver's seat, slams the palm of his right hand against the steering wheel, and orders Thurston out of the vehicle. "Give me a hand will ya? I'll rev it up while you push from behind."

Mud and gravel scatter from the back wheels in all directions. On one attempt they almost succeed in getting the car to the road, but it slides back into the groove where it started.

"Jesus Christ, Thurston, push, damn it." Jeremy is losing it. He pushes down on the accelerator and Thurston eats mud.

Thurston exerts what little strength he has left but they still can't free the vehicle. They're ready to give up when they see Chuckie's flashlight reflecting from the ditch.

Jeremy gets out and stands on the shoulder, pointing himself into the ditch to have a leak. He turns to face the figure walking toward them. "Hey Chuckie, how's it going? You gettin' lots of bottles?"

"Yup. I g-g-got so many I can't hardly carry no more," he answers, as if the earlier altercation had never occurred. "You g-g-guys need s-s-some help?"

Jeremy explains their dilemma. "Tell you what we'll do Chuckie. If you give us a hand, and we get the car out, we'll drive you and all your bottles back to town. Is that a deal, or what?"

Chuckie ponders the proposal for a moment, and then nods his head in agreement.

Despite Chuckie's bad leg and the poor coordination of the two drunks, they manage, with some cursing and stammering, to place the battered Dodge back on the gravel.

Thurston helps Chuckie place his bottles into the trunk before getting back into the car. Just as Chuckie is ready to slide in behind him, Jeremy pushes his foot to the floor and speeds off, leaving Chuckie standing alone in the dark, this time without his stock of bottles.

"D-d-damn it," he curses; mad at himself for falling for the gag. "You b-b-bastards."

Thurston, who feels a pang of conscience over the caper, convinces Jeremy to stop the car. This time Jeremy obeys, waiting for Chuckie to catch up.

Minutes after Chuckie gets in, Thurston starts to gag. He holds his right hand in front of his mouth and waves the left one signaling Jeremy to pull over. The car stops and Chuckie jumps out just in time for Thurston to propel himself through the open door and empty the acidic contents from his stomach. Thurston falls out onto the shoulder and doubles over on all fours, hoping to expel more.

Fifteen minutes pass before Chuckie and Jeremy can drag Thurston's puke-covered body back into the vehicle. They toss him into the back seat and give him a plastic garbage bag in case he repeats his involuntary actions. He remains quiet and still.

As the threesome arrive at the edge of town, Jeremy swings the Dodge onto a side street. Chuckie asks why he's going that way. "My house is only t-t-two more b-b-blocks away. Where are we g-g-going?"

"I just had a bright idea," Jeremy answers. He pulls the car into the driveway of a small blue clapboard bungalow that looks the worst for wear. Paint peels from a collapsing verandah and a screen door scrapes on its rusting hinges as Jeremy opens it. He thumps on the wooden front door and waits for an answer.

"What are we d-d-doing at Shirley's place, Jeremy?" Chuckie calls from the street. "Why'd we c-c-come here?"

"We're going to get us some thrills, Chuckie," he answers.

"I don't want no thrills," Chuckie pleads. "I just want to go home with my b-b-bottles."

Chuckie watches from the street while a woman in a tee shirt that stretches Bob Marley's distorted face across her mountainous chest, appears at the door to meet Jeremy. Her disheveled blondish hair reveals darker origins. Soft bulges roll over her otherwise shapely hips adding several years to her thirty-two. A tight pair of faded denim shorts stretches its frayed remains over the extra bulk, from which two sturdy legs taper downward, inserting themselves into a pair of imitation patent leather cowboy boots. A flowery tattoo encircles her upper left leg like a garter belt, disappearing into the forbidden region.

Jeremy struts on her verandah like a drunken peacock, shuffling back and forth from foot to foot. "Hey, Shirley, whatcha got happening?" As he leans left, his foot slips from under him. He grabs for the screen door to brace himself.

"You're pissed again, Jeremy." Shirley reaches out to steady him. She peers out into the darkness of the street and sees Chuckie leaning against the Dodge. "Why'd you bring him?" She squints her eyes and notices that his coveralls are covered in caked mud with pieces of grass sticking out of it.

"If you're visiting me for what I think you're here for, you have to leave Chuckie outside. I can't have you both in here. Besides I just cleaned the place up and … well, Chuckie gives me the creeps, you know what I mean?"

Jeremy moves closer to Shirley. He pecks a kiss on her cheek, and she pecks back. He turns to the street where Chuckie waits for instructions. "Chuckie!" he shouts. "You stay with the car just in case Thurston has to get out to puke again. Don't let him throw up in my car. I'm just going in to see Shirley for a while."

Chuckie is happy he doesn't have to go inside. He's heard about Shirley and her exploits, and about things she does to men, and he doesn't want anything to do with her. He just hopes that Jeremy won't be too long. Although Chuckie usually goes out of his way to help people, he doesn't care for taking on too much responsibility, like being responsible for Jeremy's Dodge. He knows what it means to him.

Chuckie looks into the car at Thurston every minute or so, but Thurston hasn't moved at all. He just lies on his side in the back seat with his knees tucked up against his chest. Chuckie thinks he looks just like a newborn baby. He also thinks that he looks a bit uncomfortable, so he opens the door, pushes the passenger seat forward and climbs into the back seat in an effort to help straighten Thurston out.

He remembers his mother telling him years before, "Don't roll yourself up like a ball, Chuckie, you'll fill yourself up with gas, and it's gotta get out somehow." Chuckie has visions of all that gas being released from Thurston and it isn't a pleasant thought.

He pulls at Thurston's boots in a futile attempt to straighten his legs, but nothing moves. Leaving the passenger door ajar, he turns and runs up to Shirley's front door, pushing it open and running inside. Jeremy is stretched out on the sofa with his pants in a ball on the floor.

Chuckie sees Shirley bent over Jeremy and concludes that all the stories he's heard about what Shirley does to men are true. He turns his face away and hides his eyes with his hand so he won't see any more.

"Jeremy, c-c-come to the car," Chuckie pleads, "You g-g-gotta come right now. Thurston's as c-c-cold as a fish. I don't think he's f-f-feeling too good."

He can hear Jeremy's voice respond from the sofa. "Aw Jesus, Chuckie. Go on back outside and leave us alone. I'm busy, can't you see? Thurston's just passed out that's all. I'll tell you what. You just walk home. It ain't too far. I'll bring your bottles around to you in the morning. Just leave me and Shirley alone right now. I'll take care of Thurston when I'm done."

Chuckie's relieved to be freed of his responsibility. Without looking back at Jeremy and Shirley, he quickly removes himself from the house, stops at the car to take one last look at Thurston laying cold and still in the back seat, and closes the passenger door thinking that Thurston may warm up if he isn't exposed to the cool night air. He disappears into the night, keeping his eyes peeled for stray bottles.

It isn't until the local newspaper hits the street the following Wednesday that Chuckie discovers that Thurston never warmed up.

DONUTS

"Gimme a large double-double with a box of 20 bits." The man in coveralls and a John Deere baseball cap turns to his wife. "What are you havin' Martha?"

"I don't want no bits. Gimme a Boston Cream and a Blueberry Fritter instead, and a large double-double with extra sugar on the side. Get little Billy a donut and a Coke. Only one donut, you know how outa control he gets when he eats too much sugar. While you're gettin' those, I'll find us a seat. D'ya wanna sit by the winda, Tom?"

Tom answers. "No. No way. Too much sun hurts my eyes. Get a table over there, on the shady side."

Martha wends through the crowd to secure an empty table.

"I thought I told you, no winda seat," Tom complains when he arrives at the table with his order.

Martha counters. "The only shady seats were next to the washroom, and I'm not sittin' over there, with all of them people walkin' past us to take a crapper. Stop complainin', Tom. You can sit with your back to the sun, you'll be alright."

"Shit!" Tom says as the flimsy top on his X-large paper cup snaps off when he squeezes into the plastic seat, spilling coffee across the table.

"Now look what 'ya done, Tom." Martha wipes up the mess with her paper napkin. "And they never give you enough napkins either. They used to have them sittin' on every table, remember them chrome boxes with the napkins in? They also used to have sugars and creamers on the tables too? What ever happened to them? Why don't you ask for the china cups instead of these paper ones? You always screw them up."

"They cheat you on the china cups," Tom answers. "There ain't as much coffee in them as they put in the cardboard ones. Besides, the china ones don't have tops on them, and I always spill some out carrying them before I get to the table. I'll tell ya, they get you comin' or goin'. And another thing. How can ya tell if they properly wash the china cups? What if there's somebody else's germs on it? Somebody mighta sneezed on it. No tellin' what you can get from that."

"Hey, look Tom," Martha points out the window. "The Jacksons just drove into the parking lot. Put somethin' on the table next to us so they can sit with us."

"Maybe the Pastor don't wanna sit with us," Tom offers. "There's a whole lotta other people here they could sit with."

"Put your hat on the table, Tom. Reserve it for them before somebody else takes it."

"I'm not takin' my hat off in here. This is just a donut shop, not a proper fancy restaurant, or nothin' like that. I ain't had a haircut in a spell. People'll think I'm some kind of hick, or a hippie, somethin' like that."

Martha shouts, waving her arm. "Yoo-hoo! Pastor Jackson. Over here. We saved you'se a table. Right here by the winda."

The pastor's wife greets them, and Pastor Jackson pats the boy on the head before sitting. "He's surely growing, eh? How old are you now, Billy?"

"Seven," Billy answers, his mouth bursting with a Boston Cream donut.

"Won't be long before you start looking at the girls, eh?" Wink, wink.

Martha says, "I hope it's still a while yet Pastor."

"Speaking of girls," Pastor Jackson addresses Martha. "Where's your daughter Cassie been keeping lately? I haven't seen her at the service in a while."

"Oh, Cassie's been pretty busy with school and stuff, you know how teenagers are. She's also busy with sports. She's a cheerleader at the school, you already knew that I s'pose."

"We're never too busy for the Lord. That's why there's a Lord's Day, so we can spend some valuable time with Him. That's even more important for teenagers. We don't want them to walk down the wrong path into drugs and alcohol, like they do in the big cities."

The Pastor's wife offers, "I thought I saw Cassie one day last week in town. It was near the bowling alley. She was with some of her friends. I thought she might have put on some weight. Would that have been her?"

Tom and Martha look at each other while chewing on their donuts. Finally, Martha whispers an aside. "Well Mrs. Jackson, I hate to say it, but the truth is that she went out and got herself pregnant."

Pastor and Mrs. Jackson appear gobsmacked. The Pastor wipes some crumbs from his mouth and excuses himself for a washroom break. Mrs. Jackson sips her coffee and then wipes her mouth. "I see," she says, placing her hand on Martha's arm. "Is she still at school? Is there a boyfriend in the picture?"

Martha shrugs her shoulders. "I guess there had to be some boy to get herself pregnant like that, but God only knows who it is. She don't tell me nothin' anymore. Probly one of 'em young hooligans she hangs about with down at the bowlin' alley. I wouldn't a wanted none of 'em bein' my son-in-law, that's a fact."

"If you'd like, Martha, and if it's OK with Tom, the Pastor and I could have a talk with Cassie. A little faith in the Lord can't hurt." She pats Martha's arm. "Speak of the Lord and surely he'll appear. Here comes my husband now. I guess we'll be moving on." She picks up her purse. "Nice talking to you folks. God Bless."

Martha hides her mouth with her hand and whispers to Tom, "That's the first time the Lord ever appeared comin' from the washroom at the donut shop."

Meanwhile, back at the counter, "One large double-double." "Next?" "Two extra-large blacks and a fritter." "Next?" "One large double-double." "Next?" "Two extra-large blacks and a box of sour cream bits." "Next?" "One large double-double." "Next?" "Two extra-large blacks." "Next? …"

JACK AND THE LEGION SOUND

Jack is a bricklayer. He calculates that his calloused hands have laid more than five million bricks in his career. Five million bricks laid one above the other, each one slamming against his mortar-encrusted fingers and thumbs. The thumb on Jack's left hand measures more than an inch and a half across, his right thumb slightly less; his fingers average a width of one inch apiece.

Like clockwork, every Saturday night, Jack snaps into his red suspenders, and dons a 1920's 'jazz-age' straw hat that rests tilted against his ageing head, all to play piano at the Quagmire Legion.

With his world weary hands, he plays and sings what the patrons want to hear — the oldies — top hits of the 1930s and 40s, interspersed with some ragtime and boogie-woogie virtuosity. It doesn't matter that the old piano hasn't been tuned in years. Who cares that Jack's brick-flattened thumbs strike two notes at the same time, and the triggered second finger on his right hand, suddenly juts upward at a 45-degree angle condemning one of the intended notes to silence? It all contributes to the Legion sound.

Foam-laden glasses line up like soldiers along the music shelf of the abused upright piano that has nestled the same wall since D-Day; decades-old stains form permanent rings.

Jack never learned to read music, but he knows hundreds, maybe thousands, of songs from memory. More accurately, it's the arthritic, trigger-fingered hands, the ones that have laid more than five million bricks, that remember the songs. Even as the night wears on, and his senses are taken by one too many draft beers, his fingers always manage to keep to the rhythm.

Most nights play out the same uneventful way, but sometimes … just sometimes … the excitement of the music takes the evening down unexpected paths. Unbeknownst to Jack, this is one of those such nights. As he watches the regulars dance and sing along to his 'On the Sunny Side of the Street,' a pair of over-fuelled dancers trip over each other's feet and crash against the piano, upsetting glasses of beer over Jack's hands and into the cracks between the keys.

Jack's straw hat is jostled from his head to the floor. The woman, grabbing for support, accidentally slams the keyboard cover down against Jack's hands before flattening his prized 'jazz-age' hat with her derriere.

"Oh my God," she shouts, attempting to regain her balance, while adding a myriad of apologies. "Are you alright Jack? I guess we came down on you like a ton of bricks."

"All in a day's work, Sadie, all in a day's work," Jack answers, a shy smile budding on his lips.

He looks down at his freshly pummeled fingers and says a little thanks for the fact that he lost all feeling in them so many years ago. He hauls a long draw from a fresh beer glass and continues where he left off.

"Leave your worries on the doorstep … Just direct your feet … to the sunny side of the street."

FALL FAIR

"Whooey." Jeremy sucks on an Export A in the parking lot of the Donut Emporium. "Take a look at all them tourists, linin' up across the street at Mr. Bigg's Gas & Lotto. Can you believe what they're payin' for gas just so they can get home?"

"Them's seasonally-adjusted prices," Tom explains to Jeremy. "Ain't that right Martha? Ain't that what Mr. Bigg told us?"

Martha offers her opinion. "That's what he tol' me when I topped up at the old price last week. It's upped ten cents today. Of course Jeremy knows that. All us locals know enough to fill up during the week before Labour Day. That's a fact."

Labour Day marks the end of the busy season in Quagmire Township. During the holiday weekend, all routes leading to the mainland are clogged with the snail-moving exodus of the 'summer people.'

Trailer-hauling SUVs, F150s, campers, and RVs creep through town with stops at Mr. Bigg's Gas and Lotto to fill up with 'seasonally-adjusted' priced fuel. A further stop at the Donut Emporium allows them one last opportunity to empty the family and recharge their bellies with caffeine and sugar before venturing toward the 400 and 401 superhighways, where they challenge others just like them for a space in the lineups snaking home.

Martha turns to Jeremy. "Ain't that yer old Dodge sittin' over there, rumblin' away?" She points across the parking lot. "You forgot to turn the engine off."

"Hell no, Martha. I had to leave it runnin'. The battery's fucked up."

"Go get in the car, Billy," Martha orders, pushing the boy along.

She turns to Jeremy. "You can't talk like that with little Billy 'round, Jeremy. He'll get some kinda complex or 'sindrum.' There's a lot of that going 'round these days."

Jeremy folds his hands around his BIC to light another Export A.

"Gotta go," he announces to Tom and Martha. The door to his Dodge creaks open. "I'm off to see the bootlegger," he shouts through the open window. "Gotta stock up for next weekend. See you folks at the fair."

On Wednesday, after a two-day respite from the chaotic long weekend, a parade of transport semis arrive in Quagmire, their trailers emblazoned with massive shouting graphics promoting World's Amazing Travel Shows. They're laden with sections of colourful rides and attractions ready to be assembled and safety-checked at the Quagmire Fairgrounds by a crack team of chain-smoking, hard-drinking, cannabis-sucking casual workers, sporting tattoos and black Iron Maiden tee shirts with packs of Marlboros stuffed into the sleeves and mickeys of Bourbon under their belts.

Jeremy follows the trailers to the fairgrounds in his rumbling Dodge Dart. Every year, he works as a casual worker to help assemble and operate the rides. This year he's also assigned to operate the kiddies roller coaster during the day. At night he'll be a huckster at the Dancing Ducks Shooting Gallery.

From Friday night until Sunday afternoon the Quagmire Fall Fair attracts the locals in an annual party celebrating the exodus of the summer people, a time to show off their own homemade crafts, garden produce, home baking, and the prize animals they've been preening and pampering over since last year's fair.

There's something for every age group. Competitions for the most beautiful (and ugliest) babies born during the past year attract new mothers young and old. The best groomed and behaved livestock from 4H projects appeal to young and teen farmers-to-be. There are arts and crafts sales to raise funds for church groups, competitions for the best, second best, and third best of everything from apple pies to dill pickles, with 'honourable mentions' awarded to the 'also-rans.' Blue, red, white, and yellow ribbons are displayed on the displays throughout the weekend.

The midway offers a plethora of daytime activities for families: children's rides, a Ferris wheel, shooting galleries for aspiring commandos, and heart-challenging rides for the brave, machismo, and inebriated. In front of the grandstand, during the day, activities showcase lawnmower racing and a march past of the winning livestock.

Once darkness settles in, the fairgrounds focus on entertaining the teens and adults. A beer tent, tractor pulls, demolition derby, all serve as precursor's to the final concert of the night with a travelling tribute band. This year's features a Taylor Swift look-alike. The midway lights up in flashing primary colours and spews ear-crushing amplified music, all intended to suck money from the pockets of the local big spenders.

Friday evening features an opening ceremony to kick start the excitement. Pastor Jackson starts the events with a prayer. Jack, the pianist from the Legion, plays a rendition of Oh, Canada.

The mayor offers his greetings with an editorial. "Every year at this time we, the proud citizens of Quagmire Township gather to celebrate the bounty and the beauty of our precious gift, Canada's jewel in the crown, founded on the bravery, hard work, and patriotism of our Loyalist forebears."

"Quigmare was nothin' but a drunk," a heckler shouts from the gathering crowd.

"You need another beer, Cecil." The mayor responds, raising his own beer stein before continuing. "Every September we, the proud citizens of Quagmire Township, get our island paradise back. The tourists came, they spent, and they left. Now it's time for us to enjoy the bounty. That's why we bring this celebration to you hard-working citizens. Go ye forth and spend." The mayor drains the stein with a long draw.

Cecil shouts again from the crowd. "Who writes your speeches, Mayor, the Queen?"

"I'll see you at the beer tent in ten minutes, Cecil."

* * *

Tom and Martha arrive early with their family in tow. They walk to the Animal Compound first. Billy is anxious to see if he won a 4H ribbon for raising his pet rabbit.

"I did Mom. Look." Billy points, excitedly. "I got a blue ribbon. It's stuck on the cage. See?" Can we take Annie home now. He doesn't like being in his cage."

"Not yet, Billy," Martha explains. "Annie has to stay here until Sunday. He'll be fine. Don't worry. They'll feed him and clean out his cage."

Billy named the rabbit Annie when it arrived as a kitten, wrongly assuming it was a doe. The name stuck regardless.

"Annie is the best rabbit buck in the whole township," Billy proudly claims.

Tom chuckles. "It's a good job that Cassie didn't have the same problem as Billy when that little bugger of hers arrived, eh Martha? Wouldn't want him to grow up with the complex, eh?"

"Where is Cassie anyway?"

Tom answers, pointing toward the kiddie midway. "I saw her pushin' little Garth in the stroller over that way, toward the kiddie roller coaster.

Martha rants, "I know Cassie's really into country music and all, but I still don't like no grandson of mine called Garth, do you Tom? Ain't nobody in *my* family called Garth."

Tom ignores Martha's question. "I'm headin' over to the Produce Building."

"Wait for me and Billy, Tom. I wanna see if my pepper won a ribbon."

* * *

Pastor Jackson and his wife watch their granddaughter laugh as the kiddie roller coaster laps for the umpteenth time. They wave and smile at her excitement as she passes.

Mrs. Jackson points. "Isn't that Cassie over there, Tom and Martha's daughter? See? Over there, with the baby stroller? She's talking to that man."

Pastor Jackson squints into the sunlight. "I think you're right. I'll head over there, just to have a talk with her. She should really get that little fella baptized."

The Pastor realizes that Cassie's having a heated conversation with the ride operator. He stops a respectable distance from Cassie but can still hear the conversation as the volume increases.

Cassie's voice competes with the ambient sounds of the fair. "You gotta take some responsibility Jeremy. He's yours too. I need some money from you. You gotta pitch in, after all."

"Give me a fuckin' break, will ya Cassie? I don't have a job. I can hardly keep my Dodge on the road, especially with the price of gas these days. Besides, how do I know the kid's even mine?"

"Bullshit, Jeremy." Cassie stomps her foot. "You know he's yours." She leans forward and pushes Jeremy with both hands.

"What about all the drug money you get?" she asks. "I'm livin' with mom and dad and it's driving me crazy. I don't have any money to rent a place anywhere else, and how could I afford food? You gotta pitch in, Jeremy."

"I can't keep all the money I get from the grass; you know that. I have to turn most of it over to the man. I only get enough to buy a few cases of beer, that's all."

"Oh, for Christ sake, Jeremy. Give me a fuckin' break. My heart bleeds for you." Cassie kicks some gravel on the parking lot.

"Besides, I'm s'posed to go huntin' with Thurston's brother Alex next week. I promised him. He's lettin' me use Thurston's old shotgun."

Having heard enough, Pastor Jackson steps forward. "Hello Cassie. Remember me?" He extends his hand. "Pastor Jackson."

Cassie answers without looking at the pastor directly. “Yeah, I remember.”

“Your mom and dad are looking for you. Maybe you should join them. They’re heading toward the Produce Building.”

Cassie gives Jeremy an evil look and turns abruptly, pushing the stroller across the gravel lot.

“So, Jeremy, how is everything with you these days?” the Pastor asks.

“Oh. You know.” Jeremy shuffles his feet. “The same, I guess.”

“Good … Good.” The pastor shuffles his feet, while leaning in close to Jeremy. He whispers, “Could I buy a bag from you?”

“What?”

“You heard me, Jeremy. I need a dime of grass … for me and the missus. We like to … you know … mellow out from time-to-time after church, you know what I mean?”

“Yeah, Yeah. I know what you mean, Pastor.” Jeremy can’t believe his ears but can’t refuse an offer of easy money either. “Sure, come with me, Pastor. I’ll get some for you.”

Jeremy creaks the door open on his Dodge and reaches under the passenger seat. He retrieves a small bag.

The Pastor hands Jeremy a twenty dollar bill. Jeremy hands over the bag.

“Is this stuff any good, Jeremy?” the Pastor asks.

“Oh yeah. The best.”

“Thanks Jeremy.” Pastor Jackson places his right hand on Jeremy’s shoulder and stares directly into his eyes. Now comes the best part.”

“Whad’ya mean Pastor?” Jeremy asks.

“Do you have a will, Jeremy?” the Pastor asks.

“Naw. What for?” Jeremy responds, sucking a drag from his Export A. “I don’t own much an’ even if I did, there ain’t nobody to leave it to anyway.”

“Au contraire. I’m going to offer you an opportunity to do the right thing for the first time in your life, Jeremy. This is your only chance before I take this bag to Sergeant Bellamy. I’ve been recording our entire conversation. Cassie needs help with the baby. You're the father. Are you going to stand up to the plate and become a respectable man, or will I turn you in? Your choice."

"What can I do?" Jeremy flicks his butt across the parking lot. "I'm on welfare, man."

"As you probably know, my brother, Lawrence, is an attorney here in town. At my request, he'll write up a will for you that leaves your entire estate to Cassie when you die … even that rusty old Dodge. There will also be a separate contract to sign that requires you to provide a third of everything you earn to Cassie, including a third of your welfare cheque. All you have to do is sign the papers. Lawrence won't even charge you for writing them up. That's a good deal Jeremy."

"I'm not signin' anything," Jeremy says, turning his back to the Pastor. "You can go to Hell."

Pastor Jackson continues, struggling to maintain his cool. "I was going to demand that you do the honourable thing by marrying Cassie so you'd be responsible by law. I would have done the service at the church for free, but I quickly realized that it would be terribly unfair to her and the boy. After all, little Garth doesn't deserve to be raised by a worthless piece of shit; a drug dealer who can't stop boozing. What a combination."

The Pastor points his finger at Jeremy's face to deliver his ultimatum. "I'm calling my brother right now. By tonight he'll have the papers ready for signing. It won't be in your best interest to refuse." Pastor Jackson waves the dime bag in front of Jeremy's eyes.

"Go to Hell."

"Oh, another thing," the Pastor adds. "I almost forgot. Cassie just turned seventeen this month. That means that she was sixteen when she became pregnant. How old are you now Jeremy? Thirty something? Just food for thought before you refuse to sign the contract. God bless."

* * *

"Hey Tom!" Martha calls with excitement in her voice. "Check this out. I won first prize in the ugly pepper contest. Take a picture."

"That's the ugliest pepper I ever seen, Martha. Why'd ya enter that one?"

"Because … it looks like one of those things … you know … those things that men have. I don't wanna say it in front of Billy."

Tom answers. "He's a boy, fer Christ sake, Martha. He's got one of those things himself. He ain't gonna get a complex if you just call it like it is … you know … a dick."

He pokes his son on the arm. "Ain't that right, Billy?"

Billy blushes, laughs, and shyly turns his head away.

"Where's Cassie got to?" Tom asks.

"She's gone off to feed little Garth," Martha says. "She wants him nice and calm for the Beautiful Baby contest."

"Hope she changes him too," Tom offers. "He didn't smell too fresh when I saw them."

Ben Flaherty, the realtor, shouts from his booth. "Hey Tom … Martha. Come on over here. I've got a real honey of a deal for you'se. Ain't it about time you folks sell the old place and move into a nice sweet, low maintenance home on the edge of town?"

Ben shows Martha a brochure with lots of pictures.

"Tom, come here and look at this," Martha calls, pointing at the brochure. "Can you believe what they want for that ram-shackled old place down on Wilson's Crossroad? Half a million bucks. Shit. Old Wilson used to keep sheep on the main floor. He slept upstairs. There ain't even any heat in the place. Remember, when he had that chimney fire, Tom. He never replaced that old wood stove after that."

"That's because the sheep-dip downstairs kept the place warm," Tom jokes.

Ben Flaherty tries to keep a straight face. "You folks are sitting on a gold mine where you live right now. That waterfront lot you're living on would attract a retired couple from the city."

Martha jumps in. "You can hardly call it waterfront, Ben. The house overlooks the creek. It's not even a river. It overflows and floods the basement every spring and dries up by July. Some waterfront."

"Just a suggestion, folks." Ben, always the optimist, raises his hands. "Give it some thought. You know where to find me."

"Yeah," Tom says, waving and turning away. "We know where to find you Ben. Usually at the Queen's Hotel."

Martha and Billy trail behind Tom to the home baking section. It's one of the highlights of the fair to pig out on fresh home baked apple and cherry pies with ice cream before heading over to the beer tent.

Billy joins his older sister, Cassie, at the baby contest while Tom and Martha relax with a few beers.

Jack, the Legion's pianist, performs his ancient hits on a donated electric piano in the beer tent. Chuckie and Walter scour the perimeter of the tent for wayward bottles, fully aware that the mother lode won't occur until nighttime during the grandstand performance.

"Jack don't sound so good here," Tom observes. "I like him better at the Legion.

"I think it's the piano that's the problem," Martha says, raising a bottle to her lips. "It don't have the same sound quality as that old piano at the Legion."

"Wasn't that Cicely Black I saw over at the Humane Society booth," Tom asks.

"Good old Cicely," Martha affirms. "She's selling copies of her book to raise money for the animal shelter. It's her autobiography, whatever that means. I don't know how she keeps going. She must be in her forties or fifties now, eh?"

"Yup," Tom agrees, bending an arm to drain his bottle. He belches. "She still looks good though, eh?"

After their second beer, Tom tosses the empties outside the tent to Walter. "Chuckie must be looking after the grandstand area," he tells Martha.

"Enough of the small talk, Tom. Jack's fingers are all warmed up and we're well lubricated. C'mon. Let's hit the dance floor." She grabs Tom by the hand and drags him into the centre of the tent to applause from the crowd.

Jack smiles and pounds out a few choruses of Glenn Miller's wartime classic, 'In the Mood.'

* * *

"Grab a picnic table, Martha. It's dinnertime. I'll go and order the food. "What'll it be. Tio's Tacos or dogs and burgers?"

Martha shouts, "Stick to the basics, Tom. Dogs and burgers. You know how I hate foreign food."

Tom joins the lineup at Gino's Giant Burgers on the edge of the parking lot. Martha, Cassie, Billy and Baby Garth occupy a nearby picnic bench sponsored by Destination Travel and Funeral Home.

"Who's havin' dogs and who wants burgers?" Tom yells.

They all answer together. Tom hears two dogs for Billy, one of each for Martha, and a burger for Cassie.

"Gimme four dogs, three burgers, and four fries," Tom counts on his fingers and yells through the opening. "Better throw in a couple of onion rings too … oh, and two coffees and a couple a Pepsi's." While the order is being grilled, Tom grabs bags of vinegar, pepper, and salt and delivers them to the picnic table.

"You forgot the sugars and whiteners for the coffees, Tom," Martha shouts. "Don't worry. I'll come up and get 'em and give you a hand with the burgers too."

From the food area, the din and fumes from the demolition derby fill the air. An announcer calls out the action over the PA.

"NUMBER 21 IS DOWN. LOOK AT THE SMOKE COMIN' FROM BOBBY LASSITER'S OLD CADDIE …"

Between her hot dog and burger, Martha arranges with Cassie. "So, you take Billy back home with you and the baby while Tom and I check out the midway for a while. I'll come home around eight to look after the kids and give you a chance to return for the big grandstand show. You can come home with Tom. That OK with you, Cassie?"

Cassie nods, her mouth stuffed with fries. She pushes a soggy fry between Garth's lips.

* * *

The midway is in full tilt when Cassie returns. Darkness falls over the fairgrounds. A warmup band takes the stage, opening with a Roy Orbison cover. Bright lights circle through the dark sky as the Ferris wheel turns to the repetitive loops of 'circus' music and the midway comes alive with flashing colours and neon signs.

Hucksters shout their come-ons from each booth, their voices running together. "Candy Floss!" "Step right up!" "Try your luck, catch three goldfish for a prize."

One booth away from the candy floss, Jeremy shouts from the Dancing Ducks Shooting Gallery. "Step right up, folks! Win your honey a prize. Only two bucks. Hit three ducks for a stuffed animal."

When Cicely Black passes, Jeremy shouts. "Hey Cicely. C'mon over here, doll. Brighten up my day. I'll give you a prize."

Cicely raises her third finger. Her escort, the Chicago Bear lineman, approaches Jeremy.

"Don't I know you from somewhere, asshole?"

With three active shooters at the Dancing Ducks, Pastor Jackson arrives.

"Hello, Jeremy. I thought I'd find you here. Give me one of those guns. I think I'll try my luck. Give one to my brother, Lawrence, too. He's the attorney I told you about. Get ready to sign the contract when we're finished blowing those ducks away."

"Screw off, Jackson. Can't you see I'm busy?"

The Pastor and Lawrence score three ducks each. "You owe us both a prize. We'll give the stuffed animals to your son." The Pastor produces the paperwork for Jeremy's signature. "We brought a witness for the signatures, Jeremy."

Sergeant Bellamy steps up to the booth.

Jeremy resists. "I ain't signing no papers. You can't make me."

"That's right Jeremy. You don't have to sign," the Pastor affirms, reaching into his pocket for the bag.

"I have something to show you, Sergeant."

"This is bullshit," Jeremy complains. "This is a violation of my civil rights."

Sergeant Bellamy warns. "You can always appeal the charges if you want, Jeremy."

"OK. I'm signin' but it'll never hold up in court."

"We'll see. We'll see," the Pastor replies.

DUCKS

"I feel lucky today," Jeremy tells Mr. Bigg. "Gimme a Lotto Max with Encore. Add it to my gas fill-up. Thank God the prices are back down to normal, eh?"

"God has nothing to do with it," Mr. Bigg says, handing Jeremy his ticket. "The gas company just calls and tells me when to bump the price up and when to pull it back down. I just do what they tell me, it's in our contract."

"Contracts be damned," Jeremy complains. "That's all I hear about these days, bloody contracts. Like that contract that Pastor Jackson sucked me into signin' eh? That bastard. Now it's all over town."

"I know," Mr. Bigg nods. "Everybody's talking about it," he admits before offering an observation. "So, Jeremy. If you're in such a funk about contracts, why are you feeling lucky?"

A smile spreads over Jeremy's face. "I'm off duck huntin' with Alex Penner ... you know him, Thurston's little brother. He used to come in here with me and his brother, back before Thurston died, eh? He's lettin' me use his brother's old shotgun. He said that's what Thurston would've wanted."

Out in the Dodge, Jeremy pries the creaking door open and stuffs the Lotto ticket into the glove box to join the other tickets he's never bothered to check the numbers for. 'Why bother,' he muses. 'I never win anything.'

He runs his hands under the passenger seat and feels the dime bags he's hidden for his later personal use. After one last visit to the bootlegger's to stock up, he's ready to pick up Alex.

"Hey Jeremy, my man. Did ya get everythin' we need?" Alex asks. "I got the boat all ready to go. Just back the car up."

"Christ, Alex," Jeremy shouts, puffing on an Export A. "Why'd you dress the boat up in camo for? You got branches stuck all over it. We're not goin' to war, eh?"

"Why not? Look at us, we're all dressed in camo, man. You don't want the ducks seein' the boat, do ya? We gotta sneak up on 'em."

"Ducks are as dumb as shit, Alex. They're not one of the most intelligent animals, eh?"

"You mean, like us, eh?" Alex grins.

"Take a picture of us, Alex. Hold the guns up so it looks like we're off on an elephant safari."

"Or about to start a revolution," Alex adds.

Jeremy steers the Dodge and boat trailer out of town and turns onto Mountain Road.

"Snap open one of them beers for me will you, Alex." Jeremy says. "Where exactly are we goin' anyway?" he asks.

Alex explains. "My ex-wife's family has a huntin' cabin down on West Beaver Pond Road. It's really a lake, but they always called it a pond. Her folks never use it and I kept a key for the place after she walked out on me. Nobody'll even know we've been there."

"Yeah right, as if we're gonna clean house before we leave, eh?" Jeremy chuckles.

***

"Holy shit, Alex. I thought you said it was a huntin' cabin. This ain't no cabin, it's a fuckin' palace."

"Wow," Alex says, his mouth agape. "Looks like they've been fixin' the old place up." He points to a new addition. "That's all new. They musta come into a fortune when her grandmother died. Who'd a guessed, eh?"

"So Alex. When did your wife leave you for good?"

"A couple a years ago, shortly after her grandmother's funeral."

"That figgers," Jeremy nods, sucking the dregs from the bottle. "She prob'ly inherited a bundle from her grandmother and didn't need you anymore.'

"You start haulin' our stuff up onto the porch, Jeremy. I'll get the place unlocked."

Jeremy makes three trips hauling beer and some bourbon.

"Shit," Alex curses. "I can't get the fuckin' door open. They musta changed the locks."

"D'ya blame 'em, Alex? They musta spent a couple hundred thou' on these renovations. They don't want no prowlers messin' everything up. Here, let's pry this window open. I've got a tire iron in the trunk. They'll never know."

The tire iron has a mind of its own.

"Don't worry," Jeremy offers, instead of an apology. "I promise to sweep up the broken glass before we leave. They'll never know we were here."

After disconnecting the boat trailer, they roll it down to the boat ramp to be ready for early morning. Alex gathers kindling while Jeremy hauls split logs from the pile against the outside wall. Soon there's a fire blazing in the custom stone fireplace.

"This is livin', eh?" Jeremy states, stretched out on a leather sofa facing the fireplace. He leans over to pass a joint to Alex, who's laying on his back staring at the vaulted ceiling.

"It's like being in a church, man. Look up. There's even stained glass windows. Makes you want to pray for somethin' eh?"

"Not me," Jeremy shakes his head. "No point in prayin' 'cause I'm goin' to Hell, no matter what. Besides, I don't want nothin' to do with churches, man. That fuckin' Pastor turned me off religion."

"I'm with you there, man. What's the point in prayin' if you're already goin' to Hell, eh? It'd be a waste of time and energy."

* * *

"Wake up Jeremy," Alex shouts. "It's time for ducks."

Multi-coloured light streams through the stained glass high above the two hunters. Empty bottles are strewn everywhere; ashes and butts fill a couple of saucers on the floor.

Jeremy, still dressed in his camouflage pants and jacket, rolls off the leather sofa onto the floor. He struggles to stand.

"What?" he says in a gravelly voice, hoping for some clarification to the new morning. "Christ, it's freezing in here."

Alex pushes his hunting buddy. "C'mon. Get up, man. We gotta get out there 'fore the ducks settle down."

They stumble toward the lake, ease the trailer down the ramp and free the branch-covered boat into the cold still water. Alex takes several cranks while the small Johnson outboard coughs before catching a spark. Fumes and a burst of black smoke escape while Alex adjusts the carburetor.

"Man, is that ever a vintage motor. Where d'ya dig that up from?"

"Thurston got it from some guy in a trade. He traded in his stack of vinyls for it."

"Was it from Tubby Little?"

"Yeah. That's the guy."

"Oh shit." Jeremy complains. "We probably won't make it back. Nothin' from Tubby ever works right."

"That's all right, Jeremy. The vinyls were all scratched. They sounded like shit."

"Small consolation if this motor stalls in the middle of the lake, eh?"

As they leave the dock, Alex suddenly remembers. "Shit, man, we left the PFDs back at the cabin."

"What in hell is a PFD, Alex?" Jeremy asks. "You're startin' to sound like those fuckin' computer geeks, man. They're always talkin' about PFDs, or somethin' like that. D'ya ever listen to those geeks? Ya can't even understand them. They speak a foreign language."

"They're life jackets, man, but nobody calls 'em that anymore."

"Who needs them? They're just for wusses," Jeremy rants.

They settle on a small bay on the opposite shore from the cabin.

Alex kills the motor and lets the boat glide quietly toward the reeds while setting out a couple of decoys. He drops anchor in the thick of the reeds.

"Now we just wait for the quackers," Alex whispers. They'll never know we're here. Get the guns ready." He adds, "I could go for a bourbon right now."

Jeremy takes a long draw before passing the bottle to Alex.

Within minutes, the decoys attract the attention of a couple of Mallards flying past. They turn a 180. The hunters drop their bourbon and pick up the shotguns.

"Here they come again," Alex whispers. "They're curious now. Be still."

At the first sighting, Jeremy raises his gun and pulls the trigger. The boat rocks from side to side.

"What the fuck are you doing, man?" Alex says in a whisper. "You gotta wait. Be patient."

Several other birds cross their paths safely despite Jeremy's wild shots. Bourbon fills the in-between moments and warms their spirits.

"Here try these, man. Looks like you need some help." Alex opens a canvas bag and hands Jeremy some shells. "These are Thurston's own handloaded shells. They might help you. They should scatter over a wider range, and they're more powerful than the store-bought shells."

After a long lull in the action, the bored hunters decide to move to another bay. Alex fires up the Johnson and retrieves the decoys. While the tree-camouflaged boat traverses over deeper water, a flock lifts off preparing for their southern odyssey.

"Here we go," Jeremy announces. His excitement drives him to stand up. He raises the shotgun and unloads both barrels into the sky. One of the barrels misfires and the chamber explodes. Alex attempts to keep the vessel steady, but the explosion and recoil from Thurston's handloaded shot drives Jeremy backward into the lake. He leaves a trail of blood on the boat. The busted shotgun drops from Jeremy's hands at the moment it explodes and settles into the hull of the boat between the seats.

The initial shock causes Alex to turn the accelerator; the Johnson motor springs to life and completes a wide circle before returning to where Jeremy fell in. Alex searches for some sign but the only clue is Jeremy's blood-soaked camouflage cap bobbing on the waves emanating outward from the boat's trails.

A non-swimmer, Alex is reluctant to dive into the lake. Instead, he peers over the oarlock into the water hoping to locate Jeremy. 'Maybe I can hook him with the spare oar,' he rationalizes.

Finally, with no sightings, Alex is forced to return to the cabin where he left his phone. Once there, he tries to call 911 but the reception is bad. He finds the keys to Jeremy's Dodge and drives closer to town before succeeding in connecting. He returns to the cabin to wait.

The police and paramedics arrive with their boat in record time to find Alex sitting on the dock with a bottle of bourbon.

Sergeant Bellamy approaches Alex to get some details. "There's a diver on his way, Alex, so we'll find him. Don't you worry. In the meantime, tell me what happened."

The sergeant scratches notes in his book as Alex, now in a combined state of shock and advancing inebriation, attempts to recall the details of the tragedy.

Gradually, the pieces start to fall together. Sergeant Bellamy reads his notes back to Alex to confirm his statement.

"So. Let me just clarify some things here, Alex. You had no PFDs with you and you're a non-swimmer. You'd both been drinking while operating a motor vehicle and firing shotguns. I don't suppose you have any hunting licenses, right?"

"Never knew I needed one," Alex responds, sniffling. "Never had one before."

The sergeant shakes his head and continues. "Why were you staying at this cottage?"

"It belongs to my ex-wife, and I still had a key."

"Why'd you have to break the window then, Alex."

"That wasn't me … that was Jeremy who done that."

"You do know that your ex-wife's family sold this place to a rich real estate tycoon from Toronto. He tore the old cabin down and built this 'palace.' He ain't gonna be too happy about the way you treated his place, my friend."

"I'll go in and clean it all up, I promise."

"You're not going anywhere near that cottage, Alex. But before we take you into the station, I want to know a few more details. Tell me more about why Jeremy was using Thurston's old shotgun, a weapon that Thurston hadn't used in years. In fact, he once told me that he was afraid of guns. Apparently, that old gun belonged to your grandad who used it on his farm back in the day. Is that the way you remember it, Alex?"

"I s'pose that might be right, yeah."

"Now comes the big question, Alex. I want you to think real hard about how you answer this. Are you ready?"

"Yessir, I am. But can I just have one more swig of bourbon before I answer?"

Sergeant Bellamy looks up into the sky and sighs. "Tell you what, Alex. You give me a straight answer to this question, and I'll let you finish the bottle off. How's that?"

"Yessir."

"So, Alex. Where'd the handloaded shot come from? You said earlier that Thurston loaded that shot but Thurston hated guns; he was afraid of them. He wouldn't even know how to do that, would he?"

"No sir."

"Here's what I think. I think that you loaded that shot, and that you purposely loaded it badly."

"Why would I do that?" Alex asks.

"You tell me why."

Alex turns silent and peers into the water beneath the dock. He then stares out over the water where the paramedics and a diver are signalling to Sergeant Bellamy that they've found something.

He starts to retell his story. "It was me that invited Jeremy to go duck hunting, it was my idea. Jeremy don't know shit about hunting … just like my brother didn't know shit. I loaded the shot and I knew that it would back up into his face. I didn't even clean the shotgun out. It hadn't been cleaned out for years, probably since my grandad shot groundhogs with it. I knew Jeremy couldn't swim any better than me. That's why I left the PFDs at the cabin."

Alex reaches for the bourbon.

"Not yet, Alex. Just finish the story first."

Eager for a drink, Alex blurts it out. "Jeremy killed Thurston, my brother. That night, when they went cruisin' he went for some nooky with Shirley instead of takin' Thurston to the hospital. He coulda saved my brother's life but he …" Alex breaks down; his body goes limp.

"How do you know all that, Alex? Were you there, with them?"

"No. I met Chuckie at the funeral. He told me what happened." Alex sobs before reaching for the bottle and drains it. "Jeremy didn't even come to the funeral, that bastard."

Sergeant Bellamy helps Alex stand up before guiding him to the cruiser. "Well Alex. You got your revenge," he says. "You won't be going to Jeremy's funeral either."

* * *

Jeremy's Dodge Dart is taken to the township pound. As soon as the news reaches town, Pastor Jackson heads directly to the Donut Emporium where Cassie started working after the fall fair. On his way to the shop, the Pastor calls his brother, Lawrence, to meet them at the police station.

"Hello Sergeant Bellamy. We're here to claim Jeremy's old Dodge Dart. It now belongs to Cassie, here. Lawrence has all the paperwork necessary. I've arranged for a tow truck to take it over to Tom and Martha's place. I hoped that there won't be any problem with that."

"No sir, Pastor. I'll just get you the paperwork. All you gotta do is to show my signature to the man at the pound. Of course she'll have to fill out the changeover papers at the license bureau, but that ain't my concern. She'll probably have difficulty getting a safety for that old clunker."

"Are the police finished with the vehicle?" the Pastor asks.

"No need to do anything more," Sergeant Bellamy says. "That car was scheduled for the crusher next week … just the way she is. We got a full confession so there's no need to check for any more evidence. We're already short-staffed around here and we got other fish to fry."

* * *

"You're not leavin' that ole clunker in front of the house, I hope," Tom shouts at Cassie. "It's a damned eyesore, and every time I look at it I think of that sonofabitch, Jeremy. Besides, what are the neighbours gonna think?"

Cassie's not sure what she'll do with the old Dodge. She rummages through the vehicle and finds the glove box full of old lottery tickets. There's an unopened box of beer and several bags of dope under the passenger seat. A carton of Marlboros sits behind the driver's seat. She's reluctant to check the back seat because of the rumour that Thurston died there. She places everything in a cardboard box and stores it in the closet of her bedroom that she now shares with baby Garth.

A few weeks later she takes the lottery tickets to Mr. Bigg's and watches as he rings the tickets through. As the bell rings, Mr. Bigg shouts out the winnings.

"Free ticket … two bucks … free ticket … twenty bucks …"

Cassie jumps with excitement. "Twenty-two dollars," she shouts. "I won twenty-two bucks."

"And two free tickets," adds Mr. Bigg as he pays Cassie. "Good luck with these."

One week later, the same day as the tow truck arrives to remove the old Dodge, and the same morning when Sergeant Bellamy arrives with an agent from the RCMP to claim the bags of grass, Cassie takes her free lottery tickets to Mr. Bigg's. The machine lights up, repeating, 'WINNER! ... WINNER!'

"This is a big one," Mr. Bigg shouts. He grabs the list of winning numbers and compares them to Cassie's ticket. "You hit the mother-lode, Cassie. You just won yourself SIX MILLION DOLLARS!"

THE NON-INVASIVE PATHOLOGIST

"Time of death is 9:20 pm," Doctor Gillian De'Ath, the forensic pathologist records. "The brain is dormant but traces of wave remnants remain active despite the lack of a heartbeat. It may still be possible to retrieve several hours of thought information preceding final expiration. Starting TAPS download at 8:35 am."

"What is TAPS?" the detective asks.

The pathologist explains. "The Thought Access Pathology System (TAPS). It's the latest technological advance in forensic pathology.

"Wouldn't it be great if we could determine the victim's final thoughts, Doctor? They would help in our investigation."

"That's exactly what we're attempting to do, Detective. We'll have to see."

"I have to deliver my statement to the press in an hour, Doctor." The detective scratches his head. "What can I tell them so far?"

"The subject is deceased. That's all we know for certain. We can't call him a 'victim' yet. Until I complete my post-mortem, I won't have anything further."

"What are you doing right now, Doctor?" The detective stretches his neck to see what's appearing on the computer.

"Brain activity from the subject's final few hours is being transferred onto a 100 TB hard drive via Bluetooth. Any further physical activity while that's ongoing will interrupt the transfer of information. Depending on how clear the signal is, it may be possible to have SIRI read the thoughts in the subject's own voice. Otherwise, we'll have to interpret the brain waves ourselves. That could take several hours."

"Is there any possibility that we can coordinate the CCTV footage with the victim's … sorry … the 'subject's' thoughts in real time? Neighbours report a couple of shady-looking characters hanging around his house."

Dr. De'Ath places her hands on her hips. "That's possible, but it will necessitate additional resources, Detective. I'm sure you're familiar with those kinds of problems in the force. We'll need to call in our team of IT experts and that'll prolong the processing time, not to mention the increase in our invoicing."

"Can you at least tell me if he took his own life, Doctor, or was he murdered?" He scratches his head again.

"Or," the pathologist suggests, "maybe he just died of natural causes. We mustn't overlook that possibility. It's difficult to say at this time, Detective. There are no obvious signs of puncture or gunshot wounds. The only external sign is a blunt force trauma on the forehead."

"What caused that?" The detective asks. "Maybe his wife did him in. Whad'ya think?"

"I don't know yet," the pathologist admits, scratching her head. "Check with me tomorrow morning, Detective. I should have the download ready to interpret by then. My team is already at the scene hoping for some lingering traces of sound echoes. If we're lucky, the building structure has retained echoes from the original vibrations. They could reveal some hidden subtleties. My team is also video recording with both infrared and ultra violet scans for any shadow movements that may still be present on the walls and on the furniture. Tonight, when it's quieter in the lab, we'll hook the victim up and record waves from his personal vibration history to determine what his muscle and skeletal movements might tell us about the hours leading up to his death."

"What about using AI, Doctor? Wouldn't that speed things up?"

"Are you suggesting that I should create a false report? How dare you."

"No, no, no, Doctor." The detective holds his palms up, tightens his lips, and shakes his head. "I wouldn't expect false evidence from you, any more than I'd expect it from one of my officers."

"Whew. I'm glad to hear that, Detective." She peers at the detective with eyes of scepticism.

"Tell me more about what this machine does, Doc. Keep it in simple terms. I'm just a dumb old-school cop."

"The initial download on TAPS peels data from the first outer layer of conscious thought. Stage One is chosen to provide a quick overview of information from the Amygdala region of the brain. It captures early responses to fear, anxiety, and aggression. Through TAPS we can also access cognizant details like speech, and sensual experiences: odours, touch, audio, vision. If necessary, we'll proceed with Stage Two by examining the Hippocampus region for clues relating to the reasoning and rationale behind the activities detected on the outer layer. The whole process is like transferring data from your laptop to a separate hard drive. It's that simple."

"Wow! Who would have thought, eh?" he scratches under his fedora. "What's the world coming to?"

"Oh, that's just the beginning, Detective."

"You can call me Ben. Actually, I'm Ben Junior. My old man was Ben as well. He was a sergeant." He points his thumb to his chest. "If you think I'm old-school, you should have met my old man. He told me to finish high school if I wanted to get ahead."

"So, you followed his advice, did you?"

"Damn right I did. Made all the difference. I went into the force as a beat cop right out of school. Look at me now." Ben spreads his arms apart in pride. "Ready to retire, with a full pension to boot. He would've been proud."

"It's like an onion," the pathologist says.

"What is?"

"TAPS. You asked what the world is coming to. It works like an onion, peeling each layer of data away. At present, we only have the ability to examine two layers, the outer and the second, which we currently call the deep probe. However, they already have a beta upgrade that reaches further into the history of each thought. It'll provide us with the causes and effects of each decision made by the victim and allow us to print out a comprehensive timeline."

"What more could you ask for, eh?"

"Well, there's no end to it, really, Ben. I read in a forensic pathology journal that they're experimenting with a new model that probes the simultaneous thoughts and recent histories of groups of subjects from within a city block of each other."

"That's too much information for me, Doc. You're gonna make me paranoid. I'll be afraid to think. What about dreams? Have they figured them out yet?"

"Oh yeah, a long time ago."

"No wonder I can't sleep at night."

***

Ben arrives at the lab at 8:00 am with two large double-doubles and a box of Timbits. Dr. De'ath accepts the coffee with thanks.

"OK, Detective ... um, Ben. Have a seat. We're getting close on the report for our subject. We've run all the usual tests and have concluded that he succumbed to heart failure, caused by sudden excitement."

"Oh no. That's all?" Ben frowns, disappointed. "I was sure that his wife did him in."

"I suppose you were wishing for something more graphic, eh Ben? More blood and guts, perhaps?"

"What about all the tests you ran, Doc? Were they at least useful, or were they a waste of time and energy?"

"The tests saved us from an extensive invasive examination; no blood and guts. Thank God for that, Detective. Otherwise I'd be tossing up my cookies all over the lab. I can't stand the sight of blood." Dr. De'Ath mimes the act of throwing up. "That's why I specialized in Non-Invasive Pathology (NIP)."

"Geez, Doctor," Ben observes, shaking his head. "And here I thought *I* had a stressful job."

The doctor continues. "Our victim is a restaurateur, owns and operates the Casa Calabria pasta emporium. We have results starting from when he ate dinner with his wife at the restaurant, a hearty meal of pasta and meatballs coated with parmesan and ricotta cheese, followed by three cannoli and two bottles of Rioja between them."

"That'll do it," the detective concludes.

"Apparently not," the pathologist rejects. "During dinner he had an altercation with a couple of goons. The subject was known to have connections with the mob. The CCTV footage from the restaurant shows one of the goons threatening him by drawing his finger across his throat."

"Alright. That says murder to me, Doc."

"After the altercation, the subject closed the restaurant. He and his wife returned home, climbed the stairs to the bedroom, and had sex lasting 16 minutes. This caused a definite increase in heart palpitations. He returned downstairs and laid down on the couch to watch the hockey game on TV. His adrenalin peaked when Toronto scored the first goal at two minutes into the first period."

"The Leafs scored?" Ben asks, his mouth agape. "That must have been a shock to his system."

"True, but not the big one. He fell asleep on the sofa five minutes later; there was heavy breathing and snoring. It was an uncomfortable sleep, probably dreaming something disturbing; maybe a response to the earlier altercation."

The detective offers an alternative. "Or dinner … or sex with his wife … or …"

The pathologist continues with her analysis. "Suddenly there's a hefty knock on his front door. He's startled awake from a deep sleep. He resists going to the door. More knocking. Through the front door peephole he sees two backlit figures in black suits. He panics and speaks in Italian."

"Doesn't that fancy, schmancy tech stuff translate for you?" the detective asks.

"It could, if I ask it to, but it isn't necessary."

"The subject opens the door a crack, leaving the chain connected. A voice from the darkness asks if he's ready to face his judgement day."

"That's the mob alright," the detective concludes. "It's looking like murder to me."

"Sorry to disappoint you, Ben. You're jumping to conclusions. The victim, thinking just like you are, passes out. His heart pounds rapidly before giving out. He falls, smacking his forehead against the stairwell newel post on the way down."

"What about the CCTV? Did it identify the shady-looking characters? You know, the mobsters at the door."

"Mobsters? Oh! Heavens no. They were evangelists. They're the ones who called 911."

BECOMING ERNEST

Through the window from my favourite table at Café O, I watch as dense rolling clouds abruptly obscure an otherwise glorious cerulean sky. Tornadic gusts pummel horizontal sheets of razor-sharp pellets against the patio, forcing patrons to scramble inside, escaping airborne umbrellas, upturned chairs, and wayward missiles of coffee mugs, cutlery and half-eaten croissants.

Inside, empty tables are soon occupied by the migrants from the patio and the decibel level of conversation increases while I struggle for the right, or best, words to record the event on my laptop.

'The firmament roils in dense ominous clouds that threaten with thunderous, snapping warnings before discharging a deluge of biting shards pelting obliquely across the already flooded patio outside my window at the café. It approaches tornadic proportions. Umbrellas and tables take flight and coffee mugs are propelled like missiles forcing patio patrons to scurry inside for cover. It's a deluge of Biblical proportions. A flood of humanity scurries in all directions to escape the raging tumult, not unlike the evacuation of Pompeii.'

As quickly as the storm arrived, the clouds disappear eastward and the sun and blue sky return. The sudden emptiness in my thought process inhibits the finger-pecking on my laptop; I stare impotently at the collection of words on the screen. To take advantage of the respite in the weather, I forfeit my favourite table at Café O and stroll toward a forested park area nearby. Walking the trail usually helps to re-energize my mental cobwebs when writer's block consumes me.

A mist rises from the ground following the rain, injecting a mystical ambience to the trail. A woman emerges from the mist walking a dog. The dog sniffs my foot. I pat the dog on the head. The woman and the dog continue on their way.

I stop to sit on a bench midway through the forest, reminiscing about my university days. Life used to be so simple then. My mind wanders back to why I started writing in the first place. It was the freshman courses in English and American Literature. Those fabulous works of art were my heroin … my cocaine … addictive words and pages that exposed me to faraway places, and to explorations of my inner soul: Dickens' London; Dylan Thomas' Wales; Yeats' Ireland; Steinbeck's Salinas; and, of course, Hemingway's Paris.

Ah-h-h, Hemingway. What I wouldn't give to write like Hemingway. Ever since I wrote that paper on Hemingway's short stories in university, I've been hooked; his brevity, his economy of language. I can only wish. Of course, it would be presumptuous of me to copy his style.

While deep in meditative silence, I'm interrupted on the bench by an elderly bearded man supporting himself with a hand-hewn wooden cane.

The man says, "That was quite a storm."

"No kidding," I agree. "The firmament roiled in dense ominous clouds that threatened with thunderous, snapping warnings before discharging a deluge of biting shards pelting obliquely across the already flooded patio outside my window at the café. Umbrellas and tables took flight and coffee mugs were propelled like missiles forcing the patio patrons to scurry inside for cover. It was a deluge of Biblical proportions."

"It was," the man responds.

I continue. "There was a flood of humanity scurrying in all directions to escape the raging tumult, not unlike the evacuation of Pompeii. It approached tornadic proportions, don't you think?"

"I do," the man nods and answers. "It was wet and it was windy."

"It sure was," I agree. "And then finally, as if a gift from heaven, we were blessed with a calmness after the turbulence, a gift of relief from the firmament. The sun splayed Biblical light through ever-changing apertures in the rapidly-rolling clouds. Some of the migrants from the patio returned outside, patting their chairs dry with fistfuls of paper towels."

I turn to introduce myself to the old man, offering my hand.

"I'm Jerry by the way. I'm a writer … of fiction mainly … a novel … some short stories as well."

The man takes my hand. "Ernie. Nice to meet you. I used to write."

"Why did you stop?" I ask. "I can't imagine not writing. It's my soul, my energy, my very existence."

"I ran out of words," he says.

"That must have been a traumatic experience. I have the same problem sometimes … I suddenly run out of words."

"I can't imagine," Ernie says, shaking his head.

"What did you do then?" I ask. "After you ran out of words?"

Ernie leans on his cane and struggles to pull himself up from the bench.

"I died," he says, before his image slowly evaporates into the mist.

I walk in the opposite direction, contemplating my strange encounter. That Ernie, he sure didn't have much to say.

Upon my return to Café O, I assume my favourite table and open my laptop, eager to continue writing.

'The trail is damp. I'm alone with my thoughts. Drops of water fall from the leaves. It is warm and fresh after the rain. A woman approaches me, walking a dog. The dog sniffs my shoe. They pass. We nod to each other.'

'I sit on a bench. A man joins me. His name is Ernie. We talk about the weather.'

'When I return to the café, it is empty. Two baristas are talking. One serves my coffee. Light passes through the window. It's a clean well-lighted place.'

LUNCH

2014 - Westbrook Manor:

“Good morning, Mr. Bainbridge. How are you feeling today? Better than yesterday, I trust.”

The man stares directly into my face, smiling. He seems friendly enough, but a touch overwhelming. He places his hand on my shoulder as a friend would. I know that I’m staring up at him from my wheelchair with a big question mark on my face, and that I should recognize him, but his identity eludes me for the moment; maybe in a few minutes it’ll come to me.

“Are you still having those nasty pains in your side where you fell the other day? Do you remember?”

I hate it when someone asks me if I remember something. And what pain is he talking about? I don’t feel any pain, at least not right now.

“No” I respond. “No pain right now.”

“Good. That’s a good sign. Now Mr. Bainbridge, I’m just going to check your blood pressure, not that I expect anything bad, it’s just for the records, that’s all. We must keep track of everything these days; not like the old days, is it?”

“I suppose not,” I answer, not quite sure of who’s old days he means, his or mine.

“There, we’re all done. Now, Mr. Bainbridge, do you have any good stories to tell me today?”

Now I remember who he is. It’s the doctor. Doctor … um … oh

it doesn't matter. I do know that he's the doctor anyway. He's always asking me to tell him some story from the old days.

"Did I tell you about having lunch with Fidel Castro?" I ask.

"I don't recall, Mr. Bainbridge. Why don't you tell it to me? Maybe I'll remember once you're finished."

Suddenly there's a clearing in the dark, dense, fog-shrouded forest where most of my memory is hiding, as if the sun is shining between the tree trunks in streaks, alternating between brightness and darkness. If I move too fast I'll get another headache, so I'll stay here in the light for a while.

"Oh, come on, Doctor. I already told you that story about having lunch with Castro, just the other day. If your memory is that bad, you should be in here and I should be the doctor."

He laughs. I often make him laugh. I think he likes coming to visit me just so he can laugh. In his line of work, he probably doesn't get to laugh very much.

"All I remember is that Castro gave you a cigar after lunch, Mr. Bainbridge, but I can't remember what happened after that."

"That's because I didn't tell you that part yet."

He laughs again. "You're just putting me on, Bainbridge. I'll tell you what. Spring is in the air, and I have the rest of the day free. How would you like it if we went for a walk down to the coffee shop and I'll spring for lunch? It's not too far. You can tell me the rest of the story over lunch.

I don't have any recollection of what happened after Castro gave me the cigar. That's probably why I didn't tell him about it in the first place.

"Go ahead, Doc. You can buy me lunch anytime, but if I go into my darkness while we're eating, you won't hear the rest of the story. Will I have to pay the bill if that happens?"

"I'll put it on your tab, and they'll take it out of your pension money. How's that?"

"I wouldn't know it if they did."

* * *

1972 - Spin & Rinse Laundromat:

While tossing my load of laundry into the washing machine, a woman arrives and assumes the machine next to mine. We nod politely and return to our chores. I toss in a couple of quarters and push the START button.

Once seated, I watch as she loads two machines. She's possibly in her late-30s. Her full-length, loose-fitting dress, adorned with embroidered Mayan patterns, leaves enough space from the floor for her Birkenstocks to peek out. Her toenails are a deep maroon but not freshly painted; there are some cracks. Long, heat-crinkled brownish hair with natural grey strands splays to the right side of her face allowing her left ear to display a dominant Yin Yang earring, possibly purchased from a folk festival vendor. A matching pewter bracelet adorns her left wrist as she combs her hair with her fingers. I'm moderately attracted to her.

I pick up my pocketbook, Dickens' Tale of Two Cities,' and begin reading, with occasional glances over my book in her direction.

She sits on a chair located two away from mine and picks up a book from her laundry basket.

Aside from the ambient whirring and chugging of the laundry machines, there is an acceptable level of silence.

"You should really separate the whites and the darks, you know," the woman's voice suggests. She peers from above her pocketbook through the lenses of wire-rimmed John Lennon reading glasses.

"I'm sorry?" I ask, looking up, as if to suggest she repeat herself.

"Your laundry," she repeats. "You mixed the whites and the darks. The colours will all run together."

"Oh that," I respond, twisting my head. "Most of my clothes are either grey, khaki, or 'brindle-shit-brown' shades. Besides, they're all pretty well-worn and washed. I don't think there's much dye left in them to run."

The woman nods, with an 'I know what you mean,' facial expression, and returns to her book.

During our reading silence, a bell sounds. We both look up from our pocketbooks.

"Is that your machine or mine?" she asks.

"It looks like it's mine." I jump up to haul my wet laundry into the nearest dryer and throw some coins into the slot.

"Excuse me sir, you might want this," she offers in a friendly tone, passing me a bookmark. "It dropped on the floor when you stood up."

"Oh shit. Now I don't know where I left off." I pause, looking toward the woman. "I'm sorry. I should be more thankful."

"Are you a Dickens fan, by any chance?" she asks, waving her own copy of 'Tale of Two Cities' for me to see.

"Wow. What are the odds of that?" I respond, my eyes wide in surprise. "There can't be more than a dozen people in the entire city reading this book at any given time."

"Are you a dedicated fan or an occasional reader?" she pries, adding, "I've lost count the number of times *I've* read it. How about you?"

While I answer, she finger-twists her hair.

"Oh, nothing like that, I'm afraid. A friend told me that I should read this book, so I found a copy in the used bookstore for two bucks."

"Oh, it's quite a read. Some claim it to be the greatest novel ever written."

"It was the best of times, it was the worst of times," I quote from memory. "I love that opening paragraph."

"You should memorize the entire paragraph. It's as meaningful today as it was when it was written."

I look at my copy and turn it over. "It looks pretty old, doesn't it? I guess the value is in the inscription. Somebody must have given it to someone they loved at one time. Check this out. It has to be worth at least two bucks for the inscription alone, don't you think?"

She reads aloud, "To my dearest Jonathan, in celebration of our first night together, and of the very moment we became one. With eternal love ..." She places her hand over her mouth. "Oh my God. I don't believe it."

"Is there something wrong?" I ask.

"Look at this." She returns my book, pointing to the inscription. "It says Alyssa. That's my name. I wrote this, many years ago. Oh my God, this is so embarrassing."

A blush rises across her face.

"I think it's beautiful," I offer. "You must really have been in love with this guy to write something as revealing and touching as that." I pause, watching her blush. "I think your Jonathan was a very lucky man."

A smile broadens her face. "Do you really think so?" Before I can answer she provides more detail. "It was a long time ago, and it didn't work out the way I had hoped. In fact, I never saw him again after I gave him this book." She wipes her eyes with a tissue.

"Oh, I am sorry. It sounded like a great love story in the making."

"That's what I thought too, back in 1962, when I wrote that inscription."

A bell rings.

Alyssa jumps up. "Please excuse me, that's my washer shouting at me. Hopefully there's an empty dryer available."

I watch her as she transfers her damp whites from one machine to another. Shortly after, another bell rings. A lacy black brassiere falls from her lingerie onto the floor. I carefully retrieve it and present it to her pressing it gingerly between my thumb and forefinger.

"I think this belongs to you, Alyssa."

"Oh my God. This has to be the most embarrassing day of my life." She blushes again.

"Pardon me for saying, but I don't think it's quite as embarrassing as the day you signed that book."

She can no longer contain herself. She folds at the waist in laughter, the kind that forces tears to roll.

"You're absolutely right, um … what is your name anyway?" Alyssa asks.

"I'm almost embarrassed to say. Maybe I should remain anonymous."

"Don't be silly. Come on, what's your name?" Alyssa places two quarters into the dryer and hits the MEDIUM HEAT button.

"Jonathan. My name is Jonathan."

Alyssa is gobsmacked. "Get out of here. No way. What are the odds against that, eh?"

* * *

Alyssa and I follow our laundry session with coffees at a nearby restaurant where we dole out fragments of our lives to each other.

"I was at university," Alyssa starts, stirring her spoon in her coffee. "My second year, when I met Jonathan … the other Jonathan … at a class party. We were both young, I was 19 at the time and he was probably 19 or 20. We were both unattached, so it was natural that we connected. During the party, after we'd both consumed too much alcohol, I approached him about going for a midnight walk around campus, suggesting to him that we needed some fresh air."

She pauses to reconsider before continuing. "After walking around the campus for more than two hours, we ended up at my place for a nightcap. We spent two days and nights together. I'm sure it's unnecessary to spell out what we spent our time doing. I had just finished reading A Tale of Two Cities for the first time, that very pocketbook you have, and I wanted Jonathan to read it as well. After such a fantastic weekend, I wrote the inscription and gave him the book. We embraced, promised to see each other the following weekend, and he left. His face never appeared again. I have no idea what happened to him … or my book. All I can tell you is, that there's a nine-year-old boy named Richard who would really like to know."

She pauses for a few reflective moments. "That's enough about me. What about you, Laundromat Jonathan?"

"Well, where do I start? I was a shy teenager, afraid to ask someone out on a date for fear she'd turn me down. I finally met someone … well she picked me up … wasn't shy at all. We fell in love and married after dating for more than a year. Five years later it was over; she left me for another guy, mainly because she wanted a family that I apparently couldn't give her. Well … that's not entirely true. I'm sure I was capable of becoming a father … physically and all. I just didn't think it would be a good idea to start a family, considering the nature of my job. She had a problem with my being away from home so much. Wow! That's too much information, don't you think?"

"Not at all. I like people who can talk about things."

After a few minutes of silence, I offer more information. "I guess in all fairness, I should tell you the rest of my story. My wife left because she wanted children. As it turned out, it was she who had the problem, not I. To this day, after two husbands, and one live-in, she still yearns to be a mother. I never remarried, or connected with anyone special; a few dates here and there, that's all. I accept the fact that my occupation gets in the way of any solid relationships."

"What do you do, Jonathan?"

"I write."

"What a coincidence. I read."

"And I travel quite a bit."

"Another coincidence. I love to travel."

"Haven't there been enough coincidences for one day?"

"Not for me. Look, can I call you John instead of Jonathan? It would make my life much easier."

"You could call me anything you want. John is fine."

Alyssa smiles and touches my arm. "There's one other thing that would make my life more enjoyable. I know that if I wait for you, it'll never happen, so here goes. Why don't we get together for lunch sometime soon? Am I being too assertive for you?"

"Not at all." I flip through my calendar. "How about next Thursday at noon, for lunch?"

"That sounds good but I'll confirm it. How can I get in touch with you?"

I hand her my business card and Alyssa returns the favour.

I scan her card. "No wonder you read. You're a professor of English Literature, Doctor Alyssa Peddlestone. Do you also write, Doctor Peddlestone?"

She chuckles. "I try, but nothing comes out that's very satisfying; mostly critiques and some personal reflections that no one else wants to read."

"Let me read some of it. Aside from writing, I also read. What a coincidence, eh?"

Alyssa laughs. "I don't know. My stuff is pretty personal. I'll have to think about it."

"What can be more personal than what you've already told me today?"

"Oh-h-h, quite a bit. My writing has more extreme emotions than I care to talk about to a stranger; no offence John, but you are still a stranger. I really must be getting along. There are a million things to take care of. I look forward to having lunch with you on Thursday. We can talk more then."

"I can't wait."

We exchange a friendly cheek-to-cheek before departing.

* * *

On Wednesday, I leave a message with Alyssa's secretary suggesting a restaurant for her approval. While anxiously awaiting her reply, I remain occupied by editing one of my latest manuscripts, a short story about unrequited love between two wealthy seniors on a cruise ship sailing in the Mediterranean. Wednesday evening passes without a reply.

On Thursday morning, I eagerly check with my answering service, skipping over a memo from my agent and a confirmation of some hotel reservations for the following week, but there are no messages from Alyssa.

'Should I phone her again?' I ponder. 'What if she didn't get my first message? What if she's planning to meet me there, at the restaurant I suggested? What if she just forgot about it? What if she changed her mind and doesn't want to get involved?'

When I return to the bedroom from my shower, there's a new message on my answering machine.

"Hello John? It's Alyssa. Listen, I have a faculty meeting that I just can't get out of. I'm afraid that I can't go to lunch with you today. Can we arrange something for next week instead? Sorry for this. I was so looking forward to it. Call me."

I'm disappointed. I was looking forward to our lunch, and to sharing some intelligent conversation with such an interesting and attractive woman. I call back later in the day, hoping to catch her after her meeting, but receive only an invitation to leave a message.

"Hello Alyssa, it's John. I'm sorry we couldn't get together today. Unfortunately, next week is also out of the question. I'll be in Costa Rica doing some research for a story I'm working on. Maybe two weeks after that will work. I'll pencil in the Thursday of that week, unless of course, you have another faculty meeting. Did you receive my voice message from yesterday? I suggested a quaint, out-of-the-way place that I go to often, at least whenever I'm in town. I think you'll like it. Let me know. Oh, before I forget, I've almost finished reading A Tale of Two Cities. I look forward to discussing it with you. Ciao."

My departure from Costa Rica is delayed by a week so I call Alyssa from the hotel only to hear her taped voice, "You've reached Doctor Peddlestone in the English Department. I'm out of the office. Please leave a message and I'll return your call."

"Hi, Alyssa. It's John. I'm still in Costa Rica. Can we reschedule for next Thursday? I'll call when I arrive back in Toronto. Ciao."

* * *

1972 - 2014:

For various reasons from both of us, Alyssa and I continue to cancel and reschedule our lunch appointments until the space between our messages widens, from one week to two, from one month to three, until they cease altogether.

Occasionally, possibly once a year, when I'm passing through Toronto, I leave a message just to say hello. On one occasion, I dictate the entire first paragraph from A Tale of Two Cities on her voice mail.

She responds on my voicemail in a friendly emotional voice. "Thank you so much, John. That was wonderful. I'm impressed. Did you read it, or did you recite it from memory? I'd like to share some of my personal writing with you, as soon as we can get together."

After three years, I arrive at the university and visit her office but I'm confronted with a closed door and a sign outlining her available office hours, none of which correspond to my travel schedule. I place my dog-eared copy of A Tale of Two Cities and a hastily drafted note on the back of my business card into an envelope asking for essay submissions taped to her office door, "I was here, you weren't. I'm in town until Friday. Call me. Let's have lunch."

Alyssa finally responds on Monday morning. "Hi Laundromat Jonathan. I just returned from a conference and received your message. That was thoughtful of you to leave the copy of Dickens. Thank you so much."

Alyssa continues to leave messages with my answering service, but I'm constantly on the move: London, Havana, San Francisco. It seems that she's always one destination behind me.

Gradually, our lives follow separate paths until she becomes a fleeting thought in my memory.

Occasionally, I wonder what ever happened to that professor, what was her name? Is it possible that she asks from time to time, "I wonder where in the world Laundromat Jonathan is today?"

* * *

2014 - Westbrook Manor:

"It's a wonderful spring morning isn't it, Mr. Bainbridge?" the doctor says to me while pushing my wheelchair through the garden and out to the street.

The Doctor points out the blossoms and the fresh flowers to me, but I never really cared about gardens. It is nice to be away from Westbrook Manor for a while, so I accommodate him by agreeing that spring is in the air. By the time we arrive at the restaurant, I've fallen rapidly into the darker, foggier place, from which I have great difficulty drawing on my memory. I know I'm being taken somewhere, but to where I have little comprehension.

The man controlling my wheelchair is gabbing on about something and I comprehend just enough to nod or to mumble some incoherent sound. He places me at a table on the patio, of that I am certain, but there is another person, a woman, seated there along with the man who pushed my wheelchair here. I stare at her without any outward acknowledgment. The man points to the woman and tells me something; I smile. The woman takes my hand and shakes it; I smile again.

I hear her say, "Hello Mr. Bainbridge," but the rest of the conversation is garbled, absorbed by the fog. I stare at them while they talk between themselves. I feel my thoughts meandering in and out of consciousness. Gradually the fog lifts slightly, just enough to allow beams of light to pass through the trees of the forest.

"Are you with us, Mr. Bainbridge?" the man asks. Would you like a sandwich, or maybe a soup and salad?"

I offer to shake his hand. "Doctor Livingstone, I presume."

He laughs and turns to the woman. "I told you mother; he has an incredible sense of humour; and you should hear the stories he tells."

The Doctor turns to me and asks if I would tell his mother the story of having lunch with Fidel Castro. I look at the woman. She is staring directly at me. I stare back but turn my eyes away from hers.

"Yes, Mr. Bainbridge," the woman says, nodding her head. "I would love to hear the stories from your many years of travelling. You must have had such a wonderful life. Tell me about it."

She places her hands on mine and I feel how warm they are. I look into her eyes.

"My life? What was it really like? Well, let me tell you. It was the best of times, it was the worst of times, it was the age of wisdom, it was the age of foolishness, it was ..."

The full light of the clearing burns away the fog and opens the channels of my memory; I'm able to complete the entire opening paragraph of that wonderful novel and I see the Laundromat and that beautiful young woman, and two empty chairs at a restaurant table.

The woman passes me a book, a tattered, dog-eared paperback. "It is you," she says, smiling. "Look at me Laundromat Jonathan. I'm Alyssa. When my son, Richard, told me about a man in Westbrook who had such wonderful experiences travelling and writing, and who could quote the universal words of Charles Dickens, I hoped beyond belief that it would be you. Finally, after all these years, we get to have lunch together."

The Doctor rises from his chair, claiming an important appointment back at his office for his sudden departure.

"Mother, can you see that Mr. Bainbridge gets back to his room?"

"Oh yes, Richard. Don't worry about a thing. We have lots to talk about, don't we Jonathan?"

WHY DID WE LIVE AT GRANDAD'S?

For many years I have wanted to learn the answer to a simple question, 'Why did we live at Grandad's?'

I look upon that time with fondness. They were some of the best memories I carry with me into my senior years. Grandad and my step-grandmother, whom we called Aunt, mainly to avoid confusion between her and my grandmother who died of cancer two years before I was born, were wonderful to my brother and me.

I helped Grandad work the small hobby farm, feeding chickens, gathering eggs, picking and shelling peas, and riding the tractor with him. When he travelled into town for supplies I accompanied him in his 1938 Chevy sedan with tobacco juice caked along the outside of the driver's door.

Mom, and my little brother Dave, helped our aunt around the old farmhouse, preparing robust country meals, pickling beets, canning tomatoes, and baking cookies and pies.

At regular intervals we'd take the dogs, two beautiful Scotch collies, Mickey and Lady, for extended walks around the acreage.

In the evenings we all gathered in the living room learning to play card games ... Snap, Euchre, and Solitaire ... while gathered around the radio, a grand piece of solid wood furniture resembling the door of a church, through which the news of the day came booming out.

Outside, not far beyond the house, there was a pumphouse, where the fresh cold groundwater was drawn from a deep well and deposited into a cistern in the basement of the main house. Grandad warned us never to enter the pumphouse. The pump could start automatically, and we'd become caught in the fast-moving rubber belt; maybe lose a finger or an entire arm. For emphasis, he showed us the stump of a missing forefinger he had lost, presumably from a pump belt, although we never knew the real cause.

One day while playing in the yard, I heard noises emanating from the pumphouse. Carefully, I peered in through the door. Grandad was lopping the heads off chickens with a small hatchet. The chickens were squawking and there was blood everywhere. Grandad shouted at me, "Get out of here boy." It was the only time he ever displayed any anger toward me. I'm sure his anger was to protect me from the ugliness of the decapitations, but he was too late. I still carry visions of the headless chickens around with me.

I was six and attended first grade in a one-room rural school that included eight grades. There was one teacher to tutor the entire room. Dave was only three, so he stayed at the house with Mom. With my Hopalong Cassidy lunch pail in hand, I walked the mile each way to school along Highway 24, with the kids from the adjacent farm. When there was too much snow Grandad drove us.

Only three of our family of four — my mother, my younger brother, and I — lived at Grandad's; my father didn't. The official explanation Dave and I were given for our father's absence was that he was in London (Ontario) studying to be a London Life Insurance salesman. I accepted the official explanation for most of my life but, as I became older, I started to question the logic of the answer. Sometimes, having an answer opens the door to many more questions.

During the five to six months that we lived there, I don't recall my father coming to visit us. He didn't drive, but there were regularly scheduled buses running between Galt and London, which was only an hour away.

When our sojourn at Grandad's finished, we all moved into a rented house in Guelph where Dad started working in a shoe store. Before moving to Grandad's, we were living in Hamilton, where my father was also working at a shoe store. In fact, my father continued working in the retail shoe business from the age of 15 until he retired at 70, except for the few months we lived at Grandad's.

For most of my life, I accepted the official explanation. Why wouldn't I? However, when Dad passed away in 1997, I wanted to know more about him; he was no longer around to answer the big questions. I remember asking Mom on several occasions about the time we lived at Grandad's but received only the official response.

"Why didn't he come to visit us? I'd ask her."

"I guess he was kept very busy in London."

"Why didn't he start selling life insurance, then?"

"He didn't like it."

"Then why did he stay for months."

"I don't know."

Mom lived to the grand age of 102. As her cognizant abilities were gradually escaping her, it became more urgent for me to find the answer to this burning question. She was, after all, the only remaining knowledge-storehouse of her generation. It would be up to me to continue the tradition, and to do so, meant that I should have the knowledge. Despite her failing memory for current and recent events, she could ramble on for hours about long-ago experiences.

"Mom, do you remember when we lived at Grandad's house. Remember when I used to walk to that old country school?"

"Yes, I do," she nodded. "You enjoyed living there. You went to a one-room school and played with the neighbour boys at the farm next door. You used to play with Mickey and Lady, those beautiful collies, do you remember? I was always removing their long hair from your clothes."

"Why wasn't Dad there with us?"

"Wasn't he? I don't remember. Was Dave with us?"

* * *

When Mom passed away, I was left with the unanswered question, "Why did we live at Grandad's?" Was there a deep family secret that she wouldn't, or couldn't, reveal? Some promise that had to be kept? The mind plays tricks on us. Unanswered questions raise further questions and offer an expanding folio of speculative answers as the years pass by, from the seriously possible, to the absurdly outrageous. The 'what-ifs.'

What if Mom and Dad separated for a while, and they didn't want us kids to know?

What if Dad broke the law and became incarcerated?

What if Dad had an emotional breakdown and required hospitalization?

What if he lost his previous job and was in London looking for work?

What if he was really studying to be a life insurance salesman but failed the exams?

What if he wasn't in London at all?

I will never know. I am however, consoled by something my mother uttered to me during her final months.

"There's one thing I can say about your father," she said. "He never went without a paycheque."

Whatever Dad was doing while we lived at Grandad's, thank God he was still earning a living.

KARMA ON RUE GOYER

Montreal, 1954:

Membership in the Rue Goyer Bike Gang never involved anything violent or illegal. In fact, quite the opposite.

Rue Goyer crosses Chemin de la Côte-des-Neiges a block before it dips under a railway bridge and enters Ville de Mont-Royal. When I lived there in the 1950s, a string of identical 14-plex apartment buildings lined one side of the street facing empty lots on the opposite side where we played sandlot baseball in the summer and hockey on homemade rinks in the winter. Behind the building I lived in, a large solitary elm tree remained that we climbed and swung from.

One spring, when I was 12, as the temperatures started to rise, and the pungent, less-than-pleasant odours of decaying grass and leaves infiltrated our nostrils, we assumed it was our civic responsibility to assist city workers in clearing streets of the ice and snow that blocked the sewer grates. With ice picks, hatchets, and shovels, we chipped aggressively at the ice until the pain in our shoulders fought back. After several days of heavy slugging, we managed to clear a path along the curbs of Rue Goyer for the spring runoff to disappear underground.

Later, as the sweet odours of fresh blossoms emerged from balcony flower boxes, we undertook another civic duty.

The caterpillar plague coated the streets and sidewalks with a slimy carpet of red and black. Cars slid, swerved, and collided; pedestrians slipped and fell on their backsides. The Rue Goyer Bike Gang sprang into action, moving shovelfuls of the slimy little creatures away from the roadways and sidewalks and relocating garbage bags of them to a nearby bush lot. I'm not sure whether the owner of the lot appreciated the mass defoliation of his trees, but cars weren't sliding haphazardly on the streets anymore, at least not on Rue Goyer. We might have even saved a few lives.

There were occasions however, as I entered my teens, when my actions were less than admirable. One of the kids at school had already started to smoke, and he gave me a butt to try. We didn't have any matches, but for some unexplainable reason, I did have my magnifying glass in the rear pocket of my Levis, the same one I used for my stamp collection. I discovered that it was possible to light the cigarette by carefully aligning the sun's rays and the end of the butt through my magnifying glass. It was the first smoke of my entire life, resulting in deep coughs and nicotine-soiled nostrils. Maybe, if I hadn't had my magnifying glass with me I would never have taken up the habit.

My first smoke coincided with the caterpillar plague. I experimented further with the magic of the magnifying glass by focusing the sun's rays onto one of the poor creatures, an act I am not proud of. It is, regrettably, a part of my history.

Karma eventually paid me back for having extinguished a living being.

Hockey, being the physical game that it is, and through emulation of my heroes, I indulged in less than proud entanglements with my hockey-driven 'friends.' There were two brothers, Michael and Peter, who arrived on Rue Goyer from Virginia. Their father, a US Naval Officer, was studying ophthalmology at the University of Montreal.

We, the kids from Rue Goyer, were playing hockey on a homemade rink against the kids from Mackenzie Street; I was in goal. Peter, the younger of the Virginian brothers, became upset about the four goals I had let pass beyond my Eaton's 'catalogue-padded' stockings. In the final minutes of the game, he chose to let his feelings known by attacking me and grinding my face down against the ice. I felt the left side of my face smash against the surface several times before his older brother removed him to a neutral corner of the rink.

My mother, upon seeing the darkening goose egg under my eye, and the evidence of broken blood vessels in the pupil, called the parents of my nemesis to complain. Within minutes, Peter's father arrived with his portable ophthalmologist's toolkit to assess the damage. The student eye surgeon's diagnosis was that nothing serious had been damaged.

"Oh, thank God," my mother responded. She always respected the opinions of anyone carrying a toolkit, like doctors, plumbers, and mechanics. Peter's family returned to Virginia the following summer.

Years later, while in my late-40s, when my vision became seriously impaired, an ophthalmologist determined that most of my problems were directly related to a childhood injury. To this day, in my 80s, I am continuously plagued with vision issues. Thank you Peter, for providing me with a lifetime of blindness anxiety.

My sincere apologies, however, to the innocent caterpillar.

In recent years, it occurred to me that both Michael and Peter would have been prime fodder for the Vietnam escapade, especially considering that they were from a military family. I searched online to see if their last name appeared on the Vietnam Memorial. It didn't. I was happy for that; nobody's name should be there. It occurred to me that, with any luck, they might have been rebellious enough to return to Canada.

* * *

The Rue Goyer Bike Gang maintained a substantial winter snow fort behind the apartment building. It was reinforced with ice to withstand rapid changes in temperature and any possible onslaught from invaders. There were invaders from time-to-time, mainly the French kids from Barclay Street, the same ones who peppered me with snowballs for wearing my blue Maple Leaf sweater when we first arrived in Montreal from Toronto.

When spring arrived, we set out to gather materials for a summer fort. After several failed attempts to build one on the ground, we proceeded to install one between the heavy boughs of the only large elm tree remaining behind the building. We calculated that, in the event of an attack, we would have the advantage of beating our adversaries off from above. It became a fortress, a large platform connecting to several solid limbs with walls fabricated from pallets 'borrowed' from the loading dock of a factory on Bedford Street, one block away from Rue Goyer. We also calculated that the cover of leaves surrounding the tree fort would camouflage us from 'the enemy.' Fortunately, the tree survived the earlier caterpillar infestation.

The enemy appeared under the veil of darkness one night, not only destroying the fort, but stealing the beams and planking we had borrowed. All they left were the nails we had hammered into the tree limbs. The assumption was that the perpetrators were the French guys from Barclay Street, but maybe ... just maybe ... the factory reclaimed their pallets.

The final straw for me was on the Hallowe'en night during my family's last year in Montreal. My brother Dave and I headed out early to get a jump on our competitors. By the time we arrived at the end of Rue Goyer, darkness had fallen, and our pillowcases were brimming with chocolates, candied apples, and even some home baking. On our return home, we were approached by several older guys speaking among themselves through their masks *en français*. They grabbed our pillowcases and escaped into the dark void. We returned home emptyhanded. I have avoided Hallowe'en ever since, with a brief exception when my sons were youngsters, and I rode shotgun for them.

C'mon, God. Isn't a life sentence with the eye thing a bit harsh? And why couldn't you let me quit smoking sooner? Two years less a day would have been ample punishment. All I did was destroy one small caterpillar. He, or she, would only have lived a few weeks anyway, and I was just a young offender, after all.

NICARAGUA

THE GIRL WITH NO FACE

TOCAYOS

EYES OF NICARAGUA

THE GIRL WITH NO FACE

(An adaptation of this story appears in my novel, Circles of Confusion, 2024)

Managua, Nicaragua, 1986:

I negotiate a path toward *Los Antojitos* through the assault of diesel-spewing traffic that struggles up the steep grade of *Avenida Bolívar*. I choose a small outside table under the palms where I can compare my latest copies of *Barricada* and *La Prensa* and quietly observe other patrons occupying similar rusted white bistro chairs and tables scattered about the patio.

In a far corner a waiter scrapes a table across the interlocking brick with a grating sound that vibrates my spine. Parrots in cages near the parking lot squawk for food. Low-fidelity recordings of Buddy Holly and Bill Haley rattle from undersized speakers. Despite the irritations, I accept the patio as a temporary oasis from the oppressive late-April heat and clinging humidity.

Blending *Ron Oro* with fresh lime juice, I draw my first sip. The golden rum lubricates my parched lips and passes easily down my throat.

Two middle-aged Americans enter the patio. Both are dressed in freshly-ironed white trousers and embroidered linen *guayabera* shirts open at the collar. The dark-haired man taps his chair against the patio bricks in an effort to dislodge loose particles of rust that might soil his clothes. The other man, older, with silver grey hair, hisses at the waiter to bring a bottle of *Ron Plata Extra Seca* and a litre of lemonade. His voice reveals a mid-southern drawl, possibly from Tennessee or Kentucky.

A handsome, well-dressed Latino in his mid-30s joins them, toting a bundle of newspapers and magazines under his arm. A copy of Jane's Fighting Machines falls from the bundle onto the patio. He orders a beer.

"Ssst. Victoria," he hisses at the waiter.

I wonder. 'Who else but gunrunners subscribe to Jane's Fighting Machines?'

"*No hay Victoria*," the waiter replies, waving his forefinger from side to side. "*Sola Toña*," he offers as the only substitute.

"Está bien, Toña," the Latino approves.

The dark-haired American complains, "That's the trouble with this fucking revolution. They never have enough beer."

The silver-grey American agrees. "If you really want to end this revolution, forget the Contra War, just blow up the beer factories. The Somocistas would be back in power in minutes."

The men converse about the exchange rate of dollars against *córdobas* on the black market. The Latino writes some figures on a piece of paper and places it before one of the Americans, who shakes his head in disagreement. The Latino repeats the process twice more. They look intently into each other's eyes until the Americans nod in agreement.

A deal has been struck, I surmise, and pour more of the golden rum into my glass.

Across the patio, a young emaciated and barefooted girl stares at the caged parrots pecking wildly and competitively over some bananas provided them by a waiter. Her loose-fitted dress is ragged and badly soiled and might have belonged to a series of older children before she inherited it.

She turns her attention to the Americans. Their food order has just arrived, an impressive mound of food, even in this oasis, insulated from the shortages of the young girl's world by a row of protective palm trees, the parking lot and the squawking parrots.

The girl creeps slowly through the early evening shadows and, when certain the waiter hasn't noticed her, advances to the table, pleading for food by drawing her hand repeatedly toward her open mouth.

The Americans ignore the girl, leaving the uncomfortable task of refusing her to their Latino accomplice. He motions her away with the back of his hand. *"No molestar,"* he orders. She backs up slowly, continuing to signal her desire for food.

The dark-haired American calls to the waiter. "Will you get this kid out of here? She's ruining my appetite."

"Si, señor!" The waiter replies, bowing toward the American. He chases after the girl, waving his towel. She scoots past my table with the waiter in pursuit, stopping for a fleeting moment and gazing, panic-stricken, into my eyes.

Her facial features have been blasted away, or perhaps burned, leaving two deep lashless apertures through which dark penetrating pupils focus on me from deep within. The three-dimensional contours of a nose are flattened, leaving only two mismatching nostrils that, based upon her guttural throat-breathing, may not be functional. A few darkened and broken teeth expose themselves through a larger lipless opening, where her mouth should be. Dried trails from past tears run from her eye sockets through the dirt on her sallow cheeks.

With my hand, I gesture for her to sit on the chair next to me. It's extremely difficult to divert my eyes from the girl's missing facial details while I remember my mother telling me, as a child, not to stare.

I signal to the waiter and place an order for a plate of beans and rice with a tortilla on the side. *"Para la niña, por favor,"* I add, pointing toward the young girl.

The waiter shakes his head and waves his extended forefinger from side to side. "The child must go," he insists. "She is only trouble and is not welcome here."

I object. "She is with me. She is my guest. I will pay for her meal."

The waiter explains. "We cannot allow these kinds of people here because it is bad for business." He gestures toward the Americans' table. "As you can see, *señor*, we have a select clientele."

"Selected by who?" I challenge in an aggravated voice. The Americans peer above their newspapers toward me. While I argue with the waiter, the girl rises from her chair and quietly escapes beyond the palm trees and the parrots into the parking lot.

I insist that the waiter bring me the food I ordered. When it finally arrives, I take it to the parking lot where the girl is seated on a curb. Kneeling beside her, I offer her the food and attempt to speak to her, but she doesn't respond. She consumes the food quickly without hesitation, noisily gulping it down before someone can take it away.

Returning to my table on the patio I pour an unmeasured quantity of rum. It goes down fast and smooth under the evening's fresh darkness. I take three more of the same before the image of the girl's face begins to fade from my consciousness.

It's after eleven when I finally leave the patio. I pay the bill and walk toward the exit, stopping to watch the parrots consume more bananas. It's a strange world, I ponder. We stuff food into fattened parrots and starve children.

I stop in the parking lot to gather my bearings before stumbling down the unlit street leading to my room at *Casa de Fiedler*. I notice a bundle of rags straddling the hood of a silver Mercedes. The rags move slightly, and then lay still again. Stepping closer I see the little girl with no face. She appears to be sleeping.

From my pocket, I remove a fistful of *córdobas* and place them into her open hand. She awakes, startled, but when she sees me and feels the money in her hand, the edges of her tight, lipless mouth rise upward, and her dry, recessed eyes come alive.

With tears flowing from my eyes, my thoughts wander. Thank God my kids back home are okay, I contemplate, but I immediately question my thought. Why did I think that? Why do we thank God for our own children when we're faced with those who are less fortunate? Do poor peasants thank God for their children when they're confronted with rich kids? I answer my own question. Of course they do. We all do. They're our flesh and blood.

A crescent moon, thin and sharp, lingers quietly over an unwavering palm, much too weak to cast a shadow on the ink-black Managua street. I walk slowly and alone toward my bed for the night, hypnotized by a darkness that insulates me from the earth-shaken, bullet-ridden, and bomb-blasted concrete shells of former office towers.

In the deep stillness, as I pass along the narrow pot-holed street of the barrio, through the lightless gauntlet of tin-roofed shanties constructed from cardboard and abandoned Pepsi signs, I sense the stirrings of life in suspension: a rooster, crowing out-of-synch with a cycle of time dictated only by nature; the whimpering of a restless child, unsated by the sleeping breast of an exhausted and overworked mother; the eerie squeaking of hemp against hemp as a hammock rocks from unbridled passion; the dull thud of an empty bottle released from an incapable grasp; and an exhaled sigh.

Is it the sigh of satisfied relief, or of the passing of a life from one darkness to another? All that remains is the silence, a silence that draws me back into a numbing consciousness, the crescent moon, and a memory that will haunt me forever. From somewhere hidden deep in the absolute darkness of the Managua blackout, a solitary voice, *"A Dios, señor, a Dios."*

TOCAYOS

(Reprinted from my book, Nicaragua Portfolio, 1991).
(An adaptation also appears in my novel, Circles of Confusion, 2024)

Matiguas, Nicaragua, July 1989:

Rain threatens. At this time of the year the rain always threatens but now it is polite enough to permit the sun to break through, exposing an infinite variety of lush greens.

Like a serpent, the road to Rio Blanco slithers its way over mountaintops and through deep valleys. Scattered groups of campesinos dot the narrow roadside. Some plod along on foot toting heavy baskets of produce on their heads. Others guide sleepy oxen from their wobbling, wooden-wheeled carts.

Upon my arrival at the Matiguas Health Centre, a lineup of more than a dozen people wait outside in the humid afternoon heat.

A man at the front of the line has a crude bandage wrapped around his foot and lower leg. Blood, seeping through to the outer bandage, has dried during his long wait.

"I was shot in the foot by my friend," he offers. He pauses for a moment and looks down at his foot. His mouth assumes a half grin. "An accident," he continues, in response to my quizzical silence.

"Are you in much pain?" I ask.

"Yes, it hurts very much. Maybe I will be inside soon."

Waiting behind him are mothers with crying babies, a teenager with abrasions to his left arm, and an ancient, coughing man who supports himself with a tree branch.

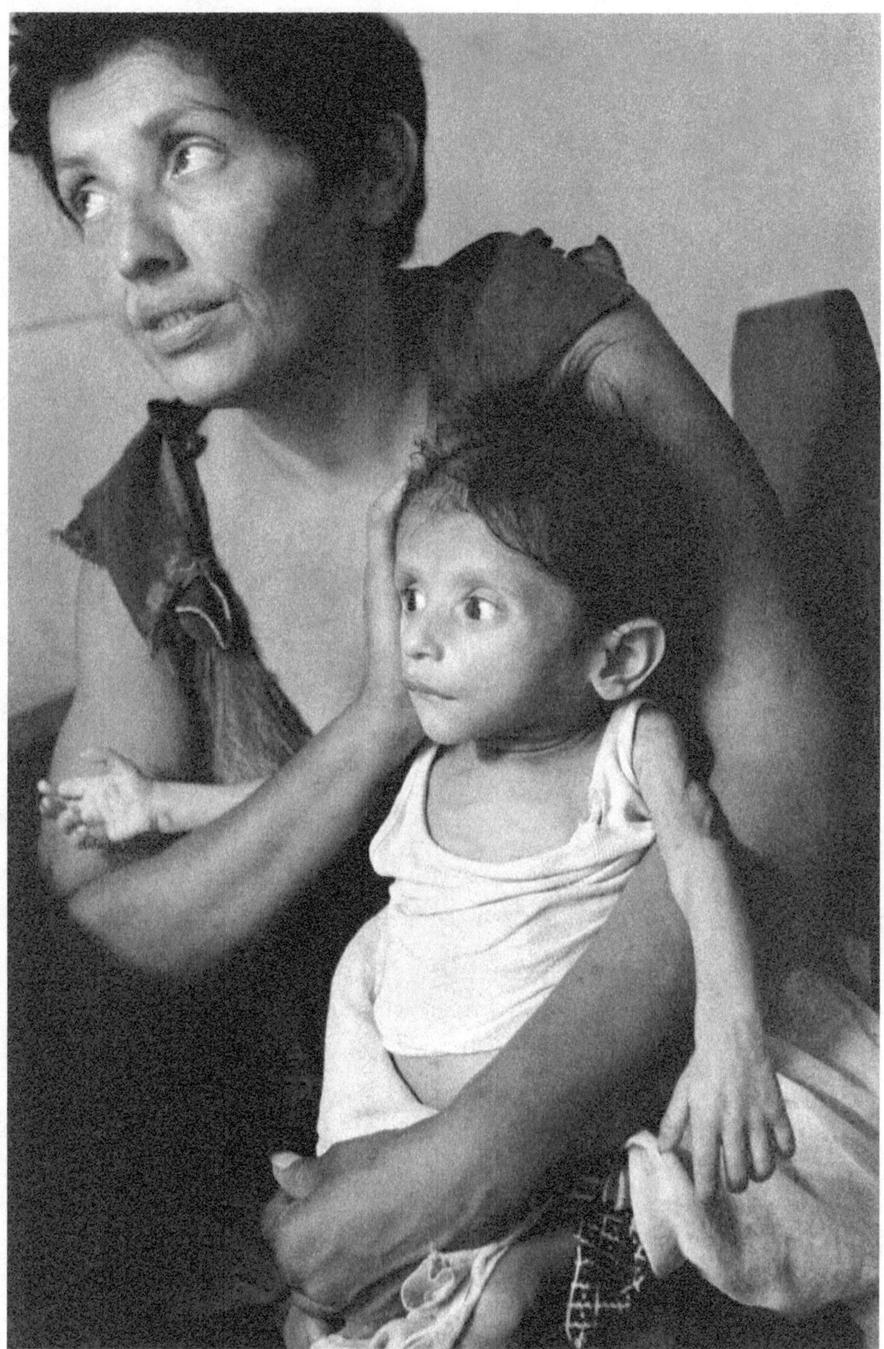

Catalina and Douglas Manuel Ramos-Gonzalez, 1990 (my Tocayo)

Inside, a nurse checks the heartbeat of a young boy. The stethoscope tickles him and he giggles. Occupying many of the beds are patients with malaria and tuberculosis. On another, a middle-aged woman waits for an abortion. Dysentery cases outnumber others in the children's ward.

In the emergency room a worried and confused-looking woman sits quietly in a dark corner clutching her small, emaciated child. The child's large, unblinking eyes search vaguely about the strange room. The woman introduces herself.

"My name is Catalina Ramos-Gonzalez. I am from Muy Muy and am poor … very poor. I am both mother and father to my four children. I work only for my children by washing clothes for other people. This child's name is Douglas Manuel and he is 15 months old."

"We are *tocayos,*" I respond. "I too, am Douglas."

Tocayos are people who share the same name. There is a special, almost spiritual, bond between *tocayos.*

She continues, "Douglas contracted diarrhea and a fever, then he became asthmatic. He hasn't made any sounds in five months and now he can't move himself around. I have another son at home who is similar to Douglas. He will be three years old in August. He cannot sit or walk," she explains.

The boy's eyes focus directly on mine with only the camera between us, not enough to filter out the power of his stare.

I ponder. 'If we are truly *tocayos*, why do I have cameras worth thousands of dollars while Douglas Manuel is in imminent danger of dying from severe malnutrition and dehydration? Where in hell is the justice?'

My vision is blurred by tears and my heart pumps with increasing rage. Unable to focus my camera, my mind scrambles, searching for someone to blame.

Catalina continues to tell her story. "I have two sick children and I don't sleep at night because I have to look after them. Last night the boys were crying all night; I think they were in pain. I was sick too. When I don't sleep at night I get sick. With help from the Blessed

Virgin and God, Douglas will be healed. Then I will come back to the clinic with my other son."

A deep silence dominates the moment. I thank Catalina and wish her well, then place the frail hand of Douglas Manuel in mine to wish him the same, but the words are trapped inside.

Our eyes, mine wet and glassy, his dry and pleading, remain fixed on each other's. With extreme difficulty, I am able to whisper to him, "We are *tocayos*."

* * *

EPILOGUE, August 1991:

It has been two years since I stood in the emergency room of the Matiguas Health Clinic, staring into the eyes of little Douglas Manuel Ramos-Gonzalez.

During that time we have witnessed the greatest diversity of world events in history. There has been the shallow promise of world peace, the stark reality of modern warfare, human destruction of enormous magnitude through mass starvation, natural disasters, and unequaled increases in violent crime.

Some months ago, at a time when any hope for the world seemed dim, I received a video made by a friend visiting in Nicaragua. He had at my request, located the home of Douglas Manuel's family and had recorded images of them for me.

My initial reaction was of extreme joy in knowing that my little *tocayo* was still alive. This early elation was soon shattered by the images on the screen that revealed the present state of his health and the conditions in which he and his family are forced to live.

Clothed only in tattered remnants of ragged cloth, Douglas, now 3-1/2 years old, sways uncontrollably before the camera. Malnutrition has caused severe and permanent brain damage. He is capable of making only squeaking sounds and spends most of his time on his back on the dirt floor of the family's one room shanty.

On the floor next to him, a brother, Alesander, sits naked in a pool of his own excrement; it flows freely from his hunger-swollen body, taking with it any hope of nutrition.

Catalina now has a job as a domestic on a farm that is quite a distance from their home in Muy Muy. She leaves early each morning and returns late at night. Her sister stays at the house during the day to care for Douglas, his two brothers and one sister.

"She is my only sister and she is very old. We are both of the same poverty," Catalina revealed in a letter she sent to me several months later. "I earn very little at my job, only enough to care for the children.

Many of our friends and neighbours who have seen the video compare the images to the pictures of famine victims in Ethiopia. Out of their compassion they arrive regularly at our door with donations of clothing for the family.

After viewing the video and seeing the photographs from two years ago, our family doctor has prescribed a vitamin supplement for Douglas and Alesander.

A Nicaraguan friend who, because of the photographs, has become familiar with the plight of the Ramos-Gonzalez family, arranged to supply them with two litres of milk each day at no cost to them. He also oversees the delivery of the donations from Canada. Catalina shares any excess clothing with other poor *campesino* families in Muy Muy.

These kinds of responses to a single photograph have renewed my faith in the power of the medium I have chosen to work in.

The media is very successful in arousing the population of a nation to accept the irrationality of war as a vehicle for peace. Surely it can be just as effective in convincing the world to repair the damage that it has helped to create.

Although Douglas Manuel is only one of millions of the world's children suffering from disease and malnutrition, he is the one that I know. Somehow this seems to make a difference to me.

Douglas Manuel lives in northern Nicaragua. He also lives in Lebanon, Iraq, Afghanistan, South Africa, El Salvador, every state in the United States, and every province and territory in Canada. He exists beneath any permissible limits of human dignity.

In his prologue to the classic photographic exhibition, 'The Family of Man,' American poet Carl Sandburg wrote, "There is only one child in the world and the child's name is All Children."

Douglas Manuel is one of them. He is a child of Catalina Ramos-Gonzalez, of Nicaragua, and of the world. He is your child and mine. He is also my *Tocayo*.

EYES OF NICARAGUA

(reprinted from my book, Nicaragua Portfolio, 1991)

Eyes of Nicaragua: dark, Indigenous eyes of Nahuatlato, Chorotega, Rama, Miskito, Matagalpa, and Nicarao, paled over centuries by foreign eyes from Madrid, Paris, London, Berlin and Washington.

Through craggy sockets at Momotombo and Masaya, ancient sulphurous eyes maintain their vigil over liberal eyes from Leon, conservative eyes from Granada, and revolutionary vision from the verdant mountains of Pancasan, while eyes of martyrs guard silently from streetcorner monuments and from deep in the bloodied sacrificial waters of Tiscapa and the fiery Hell of Santiago.

Gun-runners, money-changers, and a myopic press sit like vultures behind hawk-yellow eyes at the Intercontinental, while cyclopic, diesel-fuming Bluebirds transport their human cargo through the darkened streets of the capital, past earth-shaken, bomb-blasted shells of office towers, a ruined cathedral, and masses of cardboard, tin-roofed shanties.

Eyes of Nicaragua: hungry … for knowledge, nourishment, dignity
passionate … for love, family, nation

Eyes of mothers: resilient, protective, tireless

Eyes of children: innocent, challenging, hopeful

Eyes of poets: perceptive, idealistic, convincing

Eyes of peasants: shackled by centuries of servitude

Look into the eyes of Nicaragua to witness its soul.
Search deep with open eyes to discover your own.

AT THE CROSSROADS

(reprinted from my book, Manitou Miniss, Island of the Manitou, 1982)

The dark-skinned girl stands alone
At the crossroads,
Her long black hair
Blown by the April winds.

In one ear, temptation calls for her
To seek new opportunities
Amidst the chilly streets
And the tall towers of foreigners.

In the other, voices from a thousand years ask her
To seek a quieter place
Amidst the sweet grass
And the tall trees of friends.

She will choose to be drawn to the excitement
Of thunderous traffic and raucous nights,
But she has also heard the loon and has been humbled
By the mystery of northern lights.

She will return again one day
To feel the pulse of Mother Earth,
And under soaring eagles will give new life
On Manitou Miniss.

Wiikwemkoong Unceded Territory, Manitoulin Island, 1972

AN ODE TO JOY

JOY MIDDLETON, (1963 – 2022) photo taken in 2015

I was introduced to Joy Middleton in 1978. I was documenting social services in Kitchener-Waterloo and arrived for my first photo shoot at Sunbeam Home (now Sunbeam Centre). Joy was the first client I photographed at 6:00 a.m. She was not happy about being awakened by her PSW until she opened her eyes to see a camera pointed toward her. Her eyes and smile came alive.

Joy was 15 years-old at the time. I was a 36-year-old photographer embarking on a new project. Initially I intended to photograph many of the clients, but it was Joy who captured my interest. She loved the camera being pointed at her, almost as much as she loved her dolly.

Over the years I continued to visit Joy and take photos of her until 1987, when I accepted a teaching position at Loyalist College in Belleville, Ontario, where I remained until my retirement in 2015. I returned to Kitchener-Waterloo following my retirement.

Upon leaving the college, I mentioned to Patti Gower, the person replacing me, that I may still have another photo essay in me. She reminded me that I still had one story that I had never completed. Patti, incidentally, was a student of mine in the first class I taught at the college. She recalled a photo essay of mine that was 'in progress' when she was a student.

"The story of the young woman in Sunbeam Home," she described. "You must finish that. I think her name was Joy."

Once settled into my new place in Kitchener, I inquired at Sunbeam Centre about the status of Joy. I secretly worried that Joy may not be around any longer. The receptionist remembered me taking photos 28 years before.

"Yes," she answered, "Joy is very much still with us. I'm sure she would love to see you again."

Arrangements were made for my visit. I entered Joy's room. She was sitting in her chair with her back to me. Her PSW said, "Joy, look who's here." They turned her chair around and Joy's face broke out in a broad smile. She extended her arms to be embraced.

"She remembers you," the PSW said.

Since I returned to Kitchener-Waterloo, I've had several opportunities to add new photos to the project. Unfortunately, COVID struck in 2020, and more than two years passed. Realizing that Joy would be turning 60 in September 2023, I decided to photograph her on that occasion. (I was turning 81 the same week). I attempted to reach out for information but received no replies. Finally, I resorted to Googling Joy's name, only to discover her obituary. She passed away in March 2022.

As I write this, I'm looking through the many photos I've taken of Joy. They bring me wonderful memories of a truly 'joyful' person. Over the years, when I'd experienced some of my own trials in life, I purposely visited Joy. She always greeted me with a smile that lifted my heart. The tears in my eyes at this moment are of sadness, but they are also tears of Joy. I will miss her.

SOMEBODY TOLD ME

My father was in the retail shoe trade, so he met many people in the course of a typical workday. He was a sociable person who conversed easily with his coworkers and customers, and I often saw him joking and sharing stories.

In the evenings over supper, he told stories about his day at work. The stories always started with, "Somebody told me …"

I always wanted to know, 'Who is this somebody,' this illusive storyteller who remains anonymous? When I asked my father this directly, he just chuckled, and then continued on with the story. Could it be that my father just couldn't remember people's names? Was my father really telling me something that he witnessed, or did he make the stories up by himself? In other words, was there no other person telling him these stories; was it all pure fiction? Maybe no one was telling the stories directly to my father, but he was overhearing fragments of conversations between other people and weaving the pieces into stories. Maybe he just didn't want us to know who the real storytellers were.

Is it possible that he used this intro, "Somebody told me …," to pass the credit (or blame) for the story onto another person? Is it just a reluctance to claim the credit for the story's authenticity?

Although he never personally thought this about his job, my father was an artist; he viewed his work as a serious occupation. Every detail had to be perfect. "After all," he said, "we're dealing with the health of people's feet. You have to take the job seriously. Otherwise, you could cripple a person for life."

After such a declaration, he would begin another story like, "Somebody told me …," a narrative that dealt with some customer's foot problem or their difficulty in finding appropriate footwear.

I have concluded, after a lifetime of consideration, that it was my father who created these stories; Dad was the ***'SOMEBODY.'***

Apparently, over the years, I have quite innocently adopted a similar device when telling my stories. It's not been intentional, or planned, but I often begin with, "I once knew a guy …" or, "There's this guy who …" One might ask, "Who is that guy?"

Years from now, when my physical existence has passed into the memories of my sons, they might say that I was the ***'GUY.'***

I would like that.

ABOUT THE AUTHOR

Photo by Scott Wicken

Octogenarian, Doug Wicken, is a passionate photographer, jazz musician, writer, occasional painter of abstracts, and retired professor of photojournalism at Loyalist College. He currently lives in Kitchener, Ontario, Canada.

His published works include two books of documentary photojournalism: ***'MANITOU MINISS, Island of the Manitou'*** (1982), and ***'NICARAGUA PORTFOLIO'*** (1991). His debut novel, ***'CIRCLES OF CONFUSION,'*** was published in 2024.

Contact:
dougwickenauthor@gmail.com

Wicken's photographs, music, paintings,
and musings can be experienced on his website:
www.dougwicken.net

www.ingramcontent.com/pod-product-compliance
Lightning Source LLC
Chambersburg PA
CBHW030636120726
47904CB00006B/2178

* 9 7 8 0 9 6 9 1 2 2 8 6 9 *